CRACKING THE NEW JOB MARKET

Cracking the New Job Market

The 7 Rules for Getting

Hired in Any Economy

R. WILLIAM HOLLAND

FOREWORD BY BARBARA EHRENREICH

AMACOM AMERICAN MANAGEMENT ASSOCIATION

New York • Atlanta • Brussels • Chicago • Mexico City
San Francisco • Shanghai • Tokyo • Toronto • Washington, D.C.

Bulk discounts available. For details visit:
www.amacombooks.org/go/specialsales
Or contact special sales:
Phone: 800-250-5308
E-mail: specialsls@amanet.org
View all the AMACOM titles at: www.amacombooks.org

This publication is designed to provide accurate and authoritative information in regard to the subject matter covered. It is sold with the understanding that the publisher is not engaged in rendering legal, accounting, or other professional service. If legal advice or other expert assistance is required, the services of a competent professional person should be sought.

Library of Congress Cataloging-in-Publication Data

Holland, R. William.
    Cracking the new job market : the 7 rules for getting hired in any economy / R. William Holland.
        p. cm.
    Includes index.
    ISBN-13: 978-0-8144-1734-8 (pbk.)
    ISBN-10: 0-8144-1734-5 (pbk.)
1. Job hunting—United States. 2. White collar workers—Employment—United States.
3. Professional employees—United States. 4. Labor market—United States. 5. Career development—United States. I. Title.
HF5382.75.U6H65 2012
650.14—dc22

                                                                                                2011003880

About AMA

American Management Association (www.amanet.org) is a world leader in talent development, advancing the skills of individuals to drive business success. Our mission is to support the goals of individuals and organizations through a complete range of products and services, including classroom and virtual seminars, webcasts, webinars, podcasts, conferences, corporate and government solutions, business books, and research. AMA's approach to improving performance combines experiential learning—learning through doing—with opportunities for ongoing professional growth at every step of one's career journey.

Printing number
10 9 8 7 6 5 4 3 2 1

TO THE FUTURE

Kasey, Sebastian, Leila, Preston, and Gabriela

CONTENTS

FOREWORD

I first met Bill Holland in 2005, in Chicago, at a book signing for *Bait and Switch*—my attempt to understand and explain why otherwise perfectly qualified professionals were having difficulty finding work. Corporate downsizing was churning out tens of thousands of white-collar workers every year, but the resources available to people to help with the reemployment process didn't make a lot of sense. It seemed to me that most of the coaching, networking groups, and the unemployment industry in general were part and parcel of one gigantic "bait and switch" scheme that too often did everything but help those who needed it the most. Unemployed white-collar workers had become a market for a host of dubious schemes, scams, and unhelpful self-help books and DVDs.

By the time my tour reached Chicago, it was clear that the themes of *Bait and Switch* resonated with substantial numbers of people who otherwise had no outlet for their concerns. Back then, no one wanted to believe that white-collar professionals were facing the same economic pressures more common to hourly workers. As I talked to different groups around the country, I began to ask who in the audience might be interested in organizing for purposes of giving voice to a new class of disaffected workers—white-collar America. That's when United Professionals (UP) was born and Bill Holland stepped forward to become its chairman of the board.

Between 2006 and late 2010, UP reached out and touched thousands of people, many of whom shared their stories with us. Some had lost their homes, retirement savings, and any hope things would eventually get better. Most of the younger ones were laboring under more student debt than they could pay back in a lifetime. Many had given up on their professional careers and landed in low-paid service jobs. One of the more memorable notes we got was from a reporter for a major newspaper who had lost his job and health benefits at the very same time he learned about his wife's breast cancer.

Those experiences touched all of us in profound ways. They confirmed the lack of an adequate social safety net for the unemployed, and UP put a lot of effort into advocating for extended unemployment benefits and health insurance that would not end when one's job did. But our experience with unemployed white-collar people also highlighted the dearth of useful advice for individuals trying to deal with their own immediate crises.

Bill has a particularly sophisticated understanding of what is happening in the job market and what to do about it on a personal level. Trained as a political scientist, Bill is the author of three books and is a veteran corporate executive. As the chief human resources officer for the Business Process Outsourcing division for Andersen Consulting, he came face-to-face with the impact globalization and technology has on all of us—how it affects our pocketbooks and psychological well-being. All of that experience goes into his latest book, *Cracking the New Job Market: The 7 Rules for Getting Hired in Any Economy,* distilled into forceful, plainspoken English.

Bill understands that the world has changed. Safe jobs and lifelong careers are a thing of the past. Increasingly, the norm is for people to change jobs as many as nine times during a career and perhaps have three to four careers during the course of their lifetimes. Though the name of the game is still to hire the very best talent available, there is a gritty recognition that even the best talent is needed for only a finite period of time. Some of the most highly educated professionals (doctors, lawyers, engineers, among others) have seen their jobs reduced to temporary status.

At the same time, employers have drastically changed the way they recruit people. Rather than just running ads in the *Wall Street Journal,* companies are likely to have talent-acquisition strategies in which they tweet their openings, turn to their "fans" on Facebook, or search the rich database provided by LinkedIn. Techniques for job hunting have to change accordingly, but for the most part, the unemployment and career-management industry seems hell-bent in its commitment to the same methods that were in place twenty years ago.

In *Cracking the New Job Market,* Bill identifies, translates, and codifies the new rules for easy use by an increasingly weary class of workers. You can't sit this one out and just wait for the economy to improve. There is growing evidence that we may be in for another jobless recovery. A lot of the jobs lost during these past few years have been relocated elsewhere in the world. Others—for example, in the print media—have simply disappeared. And competition for the jobs that remain will continue to intensify. Will you be ready?

I've learned an enormous amount from Bill. He knows how corporate America works—functionally and sometimes dysfunctionally—and has thought long and hard about how white-collar professionals can make it work for *them*. He's smart; vastly well-informed; and, most important to me, never pulls a punch. With *Cracking the New Job Market,* I'm proud to share him with you.

—Barbara Ehrenreich

This is not just another job-search and career-management book. The rules for finding professional, white-collar work today bear little resemblance to what they were just a few years ago, and there has been little attempt until now to set forth what the new rules are and how to use them to best advantage. For some, the old rules don't work as quickly as they used to. For a growing number, they do not work at all. And when people can't find work, they erroneously conclude that the problem is with them—their skill set, ability to keep a job, or just bad luck. Difficulty in finding work today can be a demoralizing, energy-draining experience that saps our self-confidence and jeopardizes our dreams. People—especially white-collar workers—need help; they need to learn the new rules.

Cracking the New Job Market is a myth-busting work that challenges the conventional wisdom. It is also a simple, straightforward explanation of what the new rules are and how to use them.

I recently met an unemployed white-collar worker who had earned three master's degrees and had accumulated a mountain of student debt in the process. Each master's was an attempt to retool in response to being laid off. He hoped that more education would inoculate him against further job and career instability. But none of those degrees had that effect. Sadly, this is true for millions of Americans, who still believe in the power of education as the ticket of entry for white-collar work. Often they return to school because they are unsure of what else to do.

Education remains important, but in ways unlike before. Employers want to know something besides whether you have a college degree. This book will help you recognize what employers really want and will give the tools to answer those needs.

It will prepare you for work and help you manage your career in this increasingly volatile and competitive environment.

The president of a small manufacturing company in Oklahoma City was gratified when he received the opportunity to move to Chicago and double his income as CEO of a small firm in a related industry. Until now, his career had gone as planned. But two months into his new position, the parent company sold the firm and he was out of a job—with no severance, no bridge back to his old job, and not enough of a personal brand in Chicago to make a go of it in the near term. Bad luck? Perhaps. But the number of professionals with similar experiences seems to be growing exponentially. Even at the highest levels, white-collar work just isn't as secure as it used to be.

What are the new rules? How can someone develop a career when businesses change hands overnight, when companies send their work overseas, when company loyalty has lost its value? *Cracking the New Job Market* identifies seven rules that now govern the job market. They provide a laserlike focus on what's happening in the job market—on what companies are looking for, where they are looking, and how you can put yourself in the spotlight. You will learn how to build a competitive résumé, where the job listings are, how to prepare for interviews and negotiate job offers, what common mistakes people make in choosing a career, and how to bridge the almost inevitable gaps between jobs that all of us are likely to experience, now and in the future.

One rule in particular applies to professional women. If you are a woman in today's job market, you know that your career will likely be interrupted or affected by conflicting social roles; let's face it—women have it tougher, though men also sometimes take extended absences from the workplace. But anyone's interruptions can be damage-controlled—if you follow Rule #7 in this book.

Cracking the New Job Market also touches on some related topics, via its appendixes, such as the role parents need to play in making sure their offspring are career-ready when they leave college. Equally helpful is the essay on long- and short-term financial planning, with an eye toward those trying times when you might be between jobs. And, a final essay surveys the international job market and applies the book's rules to global employment.

There are no gimmicks in this book. Too many desperate job seekers have been taken in by promises of that "dream job right around the corner"—if only they buy the book, take the course, or join the group. The simple truth is that the world of work—how we prepare for jobs, find and keep them, and find them again when necessary—has undergone a seismic shift. Your chances of success in the job market are improved considerably if you understand these changes and know how to use them to your advantage.

I invite you to comment on the material here and share resources and ideas with other job seekers and career changers. Visit my website at www.crackingthe newjobmarket.com. Depending on your feedback, I will add courses, products, and other resources designed to help you and others crack the new job market.

Acknowledgments

I owe a great deal to many people, especially my siblings (Ruth, June, and Bob), who offered thoughtful suggestions and support throughout this project. The same is true of my sons and their spouses (Todd and Carol, Jaime and Keisha) as well as my niece Laura. In no particular order of magnitude of debt or gratitude, I would also like to thank Jess Womack, Julie Beckett, Tom Luce, John Paine of John Paine Editorial Services, John Talbot of Talbot Fortune Agency, Abby Kraus of Abby Kraus PR, Dan Gross, Marilyn Ross, Ellen Kadin and her team at AMACOM, and others too numerous to mention.

Also, I give special thanks to my good friend Barbara Ehrenreich, who took time out of her busy schedule to write the foreword.

Finally, I thank my wife, Claudia, without whose gentle touch and loving encouragement none of this would have been possible.

CRACKING THE NEW JOB MARKET

RULE

Always Demonstrate Your Value

WHEN BOB LEARNED that his name was on a list of IT employees whose jobs were to be downsized—a polite term for "fired"—he knew exactly what would happen next. This was the third time in five years he had gone through the same routine. He would attend a group meeting, which would be followed by a one-on-one session with an outplacement counselor, followed by an appointment the very next day to start his job search.

Bob would again be told that terminated employees should not dwell on negative emotions. Those who start on their job searches right away find work more quickly than those who do not. The group meetings always seemed to be held during the week but never on Fridays. He would eventually understand that outplacement firms got paid based on their "pick-up" rate—the number of people who actually start programs. Getting them to start without an intervening weekend improved the rate.

But Bob had more to think about than how outplacement firms made money. He was worried about his own finances and how long it would be before the family had to make major adjustments in their standard of living. He had new bills to consider, like health-care premiums and perhaps tuition for a return to school for the training required to change careers—to an area less subject to downsizing.

He also started to think about the damage this last layoff did to his reputation. Though aware that layoffs in some fields and industries are more common than in others, he wondered if employers were beginning to think that the problem was with him and that he simply couldn't hold a job. Three jobs in five years would surely get a thumbs-down from hiring managers. *They will want to know what's wrong with me,* he thought.

But now was not the time for self-analysis. First, he had to find a job, and he knew exactly what to do. He quickly updated his résumé by adding his most recent position to an already polished document. He had been taught by outplacement counselors: "Always keep your résumé up-to-date and stay in touch with your networking contacts." Of course, most people hate to network. They are not very good at it and quit doing it the minute they find other employment. The motto of outplacement professionals Bob worked with was, "Be prepared and stay connected. And don't forget to join as many self-help groups as you reasonably can. They will help you tap into the hidden job market."

Bob would do all that, but this time he would make a significant change. He had learned about a new way to look for white-collar work: value creation. He noticed that certain people had figured out that their job instability wasn't their fault. There was nothing wrong with them and they knew it. The skills each one brought to the job market were similar to those of others, yet these people appeared to be most in demand from employers. When he met them, he wondered, "What do they know that I don't?"

During previous job searches, Bob approached the task in a predetermined sequential order: update the résumé; look for positions that match; and in knee-jerk reaction, apply for the jobs at hand. He now understood, however, that the requirements of similar jobs change from one organization to the next, depending on the specific problems each company is looking to solve. Now, his first order of business was to discover what those problems are and to adjust his application accordingly. Using this new approach, he landed an IT manager's job at a comparable salary within five months.

Bob was convinced that his application got attention because of what he noticed about the position description. Besides the normal competencies every candidate is expected to have, there were key words in the job description that he could use to customize his résumé, making it specific for this job opening. The keys included the maintenance of a professional image (one of the main reasons the job was vacant), alignment of IT goals with corporate strategy, and IT policy development. These were skills Bob had demonstrated in previous positions. This time, however, he made sure they were emphasized throughout the application process—including in his résumé, cover letter, and interviews. The key points represented areas in which the hiring organization wanted value created. The IT manager positions in other companies might emphasize different problems. For each opening, it was important that he customize his résumé to address the areas the companies considered important and never assume that the same job in one company would address the problems in another company.

You should note that none of this made Bob's job more secure. He could get a job one month and be downsized the next. He would, of course, be disappointed but not downhearted. There was nothing wrong with him, and he knew it. He also had the added advantage of understanding value creation and the role it plays in today's marketplace of jobs. He is now able to adjust his approach to finding a job to reflect the new realities in the market—adjustments he would not have made using the same job-search methods he had learned earlier. At one time, employers were impressed by his familiarity with different aspects of information technology. He now understood that they wanted more. He had to emphasize how his skills matched the job descriptions of potential employers. He received a lot more interest once he focused on exactly what employers wanted, and as a result, he became a lot less anxious about instability in the white-collar job market.

The Demand for Value Creation

Those who understand how the job search has changed over the years have turned their career ship around so it's headed in the direction of creating value for others.

That's the innovation my firm has pioneered, after I'd worked in human resources, global outsourcing, and the outplacement industry for twenty-five years and had read untold thousands of résumés. When we began the process, we understood the job market in general but not how our particular method would work out practically.

We tested the process first on family and friends and then on a broader audience. The results were strikingly similar. We put together a value-creation workshop for soon-to-be college graduates from the Knowledge Is Power Program (KIPP) in New York City, and we offered a slightly different one for students from Michigan State University's prestigious James Madison College. In all instances, the students dramatically improved their ability to navigate their job searches as a result of our programs. One student commented that the workshop was a humbling experience that has motivated her to revisit her entire job-search strategy.

Dan, the volunteer research assistant for my first book, *Are There Any Good Jobs Left?* is a good example. Dan was a typical soon-to-be graduating political science major at Northwestern University. He knew he wanted a job in private industry but was not sure how to go about getting one or how to make the best impression on employers. Furthermore, political science was not a typical major for someone interested in a business career. Using our value-creation method to develop a résumé (and write cover letters, prepare for interviews, and eventually manage the full range of his career), Dan applied to fourteen companies, got eleven interviews, and had three job offers—all at more than twice the going salary for social science majors. We then tested the method on more experienced job seekers. The results were the same—value creation is a language employers understand and job seekers can use to effectively make themselves stand out from the competition.

Using the value-creation method initially feels like little more than a résumé-writing process. That's certainly the way it felt to Jenny. When we met her, she had already paid a consulting service $600 to develop a résumé. She got a professional-looking document—but one that was of little use to her in a job search because it was no more than a summary of what she thought was important about her background. It lacked mention of what particular companies considered important as they advertised their positions.

An unfocused résumé is a little like fishing without bait—if you catch something, it is strictly by accident. And Jenny wasn't catching anything. Though she had previously worked as a personal consultant on an hourly basis, that fact wasn't part of her current résumé. As a result, her expensive document was useless for the freelance marketing/public relations job she was now interested in pursuing. The job she eventually applied for and got was as a public relations consultant for a Washington, D.C.–based lawyer who wanted to increase his visibility in the legal community. That happened because once Jenny understood the value the lawyer was looking to have created, she adjusted her résumé to reflect her accomplishments in those areas. For instance, she emphasized her experience in developing short- and long-term marketing/PR strategies; her effectiveness in pitching to local media outlets; and her broad knowledge in developing a media list—all things she had done but had not, until now, highlighted. Once Jenny applied the concepts of value creation, her job-hunting fortunes turned around. So can yours.

Why the Job Market Changed

It is taking longer to find suitable work these days, and people are growing uneasy about whether there are enough jobs to go around. When you feel that things are rapidly spinning out of control, there is a tendency to look inward and lose confidence. Yet most of the time the problem isn't you. Today's job market has been mightily affected by globalization, changes in technology, and the deregulation of various commercial sectors in the United States and elsewhere. Briefly, here is how each affects your job search.

GLOBALIZATION

The world is poised for more, not less, globalization so we might just as well get used to it. Corporations that operate as global players have a tremendous advantage over those that do not. As a result, products are increasingly made overseas, where labor is cheaper. That doesn't only include factory work or telemarketing; even professional work is often outsourced. For instance, Craig was a software engineer who had been laid off for the second time in a year and a half. The work his department did was outsourced—once to another department in the same company and another time to a company in India. Some professionals in the automobile industry had similar experiences when Chrysler merged with Mercedes. It did not take long for many of the automobile design jobs to be relocated to Germany. Craig's initial thought was to return to school and pursue a course of study and a career less susceptible to outsourcing.

His strategy was flawed, for a simple reason: the future is uncertain. How is he supposed to determine how globalization might evolve over the next few years? What if his new line of work later proved to be susceptible to the same outsourcing pressures as his previous employment? At one time, most of us thought heart surgery, income-tax preparation, and drive-thru order taking at McDonald's were all safe from outsourcing. That is no longer the case.

None of us can predict with certainty what impact globalization will have on certain job classifications five years down the road. In a global world, jobs are fluid. For example, a CEO relocated to St. Louis for one month, and because of a merger, his job was eliminated sixty days later. In many other cases, new employment opportunities ended much sooner than anyone anticipated. Because these upheavals are difficult to predict, it is better to be prepared for job instability than to try to avoid it altogether. White-collar professionals need to develop the skills required to survive and prosper in today's job market, regardless of how unstable one particular job turns out to be.

That idea of adaptability includes retraining yourself in response to an unstable work environment. Retraining is always an option—just not the first one to consider, because it is a time-consuming, uncertain path.

TECHNOLOGY

The Internet may emerge as the single most important technological innovation of our time. But it also has increased the instability in the workplace. Among other things, the Internet:

▸ Spread near-instant communications across the globe and for a relatively low cost, making possible the 24/7, 365-day world we live and work in

▸ Allowed the cost of data and product distribution to be reduced

▸ Made price data for an endless variety of goods and services available, driving prices and profit margins down

‣ Reduced the barriers to entry for niche businesses and enhanced their ability to grow larger without additional cost—an important consideration for a new class of entrepreneurs

‣ Generally intensified the global competition for goods and services

What has any of this got to do with the job market in which you compete? Everything! It is like learning to make lemonade when you are stuck with lemons, as the cliché goes. That is what Heather did when the responsibilities of the compensation department in which she worked were outsourced. It was no longer necessary for her company to maintain an entire staff of compensation specialists. Near-instant communications allowed it to buy those services on a just-in-time, as-needed basis. Heather's recourse was to use her expertise and technology to establish a 24/7 international compensation-consulting firm. With a remarkably few number of employees (ten people headquartered in Marin County, California; two in New York City; one in London; and two in Singapore) hired as temps on an as-needed basis, she was able to transfer work electronically (at essentially no extra cost) from one time zone to another, to be worked on until completed.

Heather's firm was set up to service other newly emerging global businesses that suddenly found themselves in need of a uniform compensation system for their employees around the globe, which would help them remain in compliance with different national pay systems, meet the legal requirements, and abide by local customs—all the while maintaining some semblance of internal global equity. Her typical call came from a new client in the midst of a merger or acquisition that could not be completed until the deal included specific language about compliance on compensation issues. Heather soon built a loyal following of corporate clients that trusted her judgment and relied on her quick turnaround times.

Globalization and technology have combined to create instability in the workplace. Heather used those elements (and the value she had learned to create) to create her own business opportunity. In other words, technology is a source of instability as well as a great enabler. You, too, can reasonably pursue business ownership as an employment alternative. When companies outsource, they often outsource to the same workers they laid off. And it is possible to perform those functions across several organizations in ways that bring greater take-home pay and provide more personal time than ever imagined. Many people have taken this route once they got over the trauma of being fired. There are added risks, to be sure, such as having to purchase your own health-care coverage, coping with an uneven income stream, and having to continually search for new business.

DEREGULATION

The final death blow to the stability of our work environment was dealt by deregulation. Once upon a time, regulations protected established companies from "excessive" competition. But once the restrictions were lifted, industries such as financial services, communications, and transportation lost their "protection." Suddenly, banks were allowed to do business across state lines and could place ATMs on every corner. Brokerage houses could own banks and vice versa. Airline ownership did not disqualify ownership of trucking companies, steamship lines, or railroads, as had previously been the case. And on it went. New kinds of competition fueled the business drive for increased productivity and efficiency.

These developments, along with other changes in technology, began to give customers choices they never had before—cheaper airline seats, more automobiles, newly created financial instruments, more soft drinks, alternative types of telephones, computers in new forms, and so on. Many theorists have called the decades of the '70s, '80s, and '90s the "explosion of choice" era. The following table gives you an indication of how large these changes have been.

THE EXPLOSION OF CHOICE

Items	Early '70s	Late '90s
Vehicle models	140	260
Frito-Lay chip varieties	10	78
PC models	0	400
Soft drink brands	20	87
Websites	0	4.8 M
Bottled water brands	16	50

Airports	11,261	18,202
New book titles	40,530	77,446
Amusement parks	362	1,174
TV screen sizes	13	43

Excerpted from Jack Trout, *Differentiate or Die: Survival in Our Era of Killer Competition* (New York: John Wiley, 2001), p. 23.

The movement of jobs around the world, especially to India, China, and Russia, has helped those economies mature and increase worldwide competition for goods and services. If company A does not offer the size TV screen people want at the price they want it, they will simply buy from company B that will, regardless of where the TV is made. "Buy American" only works as a slogan if the product is at the best price and has all the bells and whistles that consumers want.

The increased choices for customers spawned high-growth companies like Walmart, which could effectively squeeze suppliers and offer lower prices. Meanwhile, employees got slimmer benefit packages, pensions that often ended as idle promises, and eventually pink slips—all to increase profit margins and gain competitive advantage. The old days when giant companies at the top of the business pyramid knew their production requirements years in advance, and could hire off the college campus and slot employees into positions over time, are long gone. Now, companies face an unprecedented sense of urgency in which, for example, the typical consumer-products company loses half of its customer base every four years, according to economist Robert Reich, who noted this development in his book *Supercapitalism: The Transformation of Business, Democracy, and Everyday Life.*

When you look for that next job, you should understand that loyal, long-term customers and employees are dying breeds. Instead of cradle-to-grave employees, corporations hunger for people who can create value and who are around only for as long as they are needed. The employer-employee relationship has taken on an entirely new meaning. The tradition was that of having loyalty to the company in exchange for a secure job with generous benefits. That's over. According to Peter

Capelli, author of *The New Deal at Work: Managing the Market-Driven Workforce*, the new mantra is, "If you want loyalty, get a dog."

Turn the Key of Value Creation

The ability to create value for a company repositions the traditional white-collar worker for today's job market. But what exactly is entailed in value creation? There are three interconnected value sectors in today's market: value creation for an employer; value creation as a member of the contingent workforce; and value creation as an entrepreneur. Figure 1.1 presents these sectors as a pyramid, with increasing levels of risk as one rises from traditional employment at the bottom to entrepreneurship at the top. The value inherent in these levels is interconnected because mastery of one helps you gain mastery of the others. That is, all of us need to get better at creating value for ourselves and our employers—learning to effectively operate in one arena opens the door to the others.

FIGURE 1.1 Value-creation pyramid.

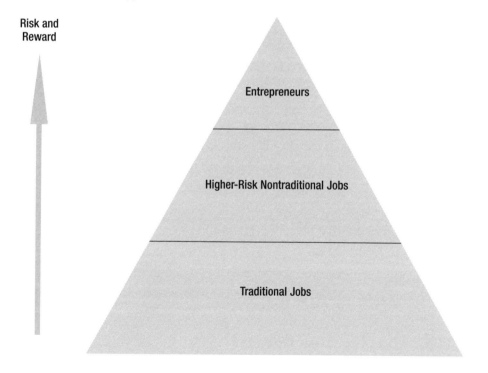

Since my first book on the subject, *Are There Any Good Jobs Left?* was published, people keep asking for a repeat answer to the book's central question: Are there any good jobs left? The answer is a resounding "Yes!" The salaried jobs with attached health-care benefits and pension programs we have grown accustomed to will continue to exist—but with a major caveat. Proportionately, there are fewer of those jobs today than there were yesterday, but there are more today than there will be tomorrow. One way to survive is to become more competitive for the good jobs that remain. And this can be done by learning the language of value creation.

Unemployed white-collar professionals often wonder if more education will make their job situation more stable. They know a college degree today is merely the equivalent of a high school diploma of a generation ago. More education, the hope is, will make you more competitive for the jobs that remain. Colleges and universities endorse this idea because they, like other businesses, are in a mad scramble for more students and the revenue stream they represent. The truth is, there are no guarantees.

If you doubt that, visit your local Starbucks. Workers there are a pretty educated bunch. If you are able, approach one and ask, "Is this the kind of job you had in mind when you went to college?" For instance, Marilyn majored in music education and had been working at Starbucks for two years following graduation. While in college, little did she realize that music programs in American schools had for years been pared back and in many no longer existed. Colleges and universities, however, were not deterred by the lack of career opportunity and kept advertising music education as a viable career option. Faced with the prospect of postgraduate unemployment, she wasn't going to make the same mistake twice and passed on the opportunity to study for a master's degree in the same field. Instead, she moved back in with Mom and Dad (65 percent of college graduates do that immediately following graduation) and took a job to pay off her student loans. What about the career? She simply says, "It's on hold."

Even the gainfully employed know that someday they, too, will be forced to test the job market. That's because the typical white-collar worker can expect to have at least ten jobs and three to seven careers during his or her lifetime. The question for all of them is, "How do your credentials match up with those of the people whom you must compete against?"

In the 1980s, outplacement firms reassured displaced white-collar workers that the reemployment statistics were on their side. Some firms even argued that white-collar layoffs were really "blessings in disguise." Former employees could take advantage of the interlude to search for positions and careers for which they were better suited, as compared with earlier ones that they most likely stumbled into. This was a time during which they could discover their true calling and could work at jobs they were more passionate about.

During a previous time, unemployed white-collar workers could expect to find new work quickly, at comparable income levels or better. The old rule was that a job search would take one month for every $10,000 of income. To find a job at the $60,000 level would take around six months. Many white-collar workers boasted that their new jobs actually paid more than their old ones.

Things have changed so dramatically that the unemployed are in need of new rules for finding white-collar work. Relying on your work history and formal credentials alone is problematic; thousands of other people with good credentials also cannot find work on a par with their expectations. The situation cries out for a better approach.

Adding to the problem, of course, is the increased number of people you are competing against. Job listings for white-collar workers attract hundreds (would you believe thousands?) of applicants. Government jobs that once went begging are now drawing 150 percent more applications than in previous years. A few years ago, Walmart boasted it had 25,000 applications for positions at just one of its new stores. A college graduate who was interviewed on National Public Radio ended up landing one of the station's entry-level positions and acted as if he had hit the lottery. Overcrowded job fairs around the country—in Memphis, Raleigh, Detroit, Minneapolis, and San Francisco—are but a few examples of the numbers of white-collar workers flooding the marketplace. If you are among the millions looking for work today, you must stand out from the crowd and stay ahead of the competition.

How do you do that? Some people join self-help groups. After all, a pool of people can find more new openings than one person alone can. Yet, there are shortcomings to this strategy. In most groups, the members do not share job leads until they themselves have been eliminated from competition; as a result, many of the leads are stale and of little use. The one thing the groups could help with—a sharpened focus on how to compete in a crowded job market—they seldom discuss.

Rather than share job leads, one group prepared a mock application for an HR position at IBM and then critiqued each other's candidacy. None of the members had worked at IBM, nor was IBM on any of their radar screens as a possible job source—yet it was considered a highly desirable employer. The "educated guess" most of them made about IBM was that they hired outsiders only when filling entry-level positions.

As it turns out, most of what they thought about IBM was inaccurate. Of the 129 open HR positions (who knew there were that many anywhere, let alone at one company?), only four were in the United States. Several openings were in India, Europe, Asia, and South America—good news for some candidates who were fluent in other languages and open to moving internationally but bad luck for all the others.

Nevertheless, each group member was asked to compare his or her own credentials and cover letters with those of others in the group. All the cover letters and résumés were distributed and the participants were to independently award points for the best submissions. The exercise was designed to focus these job seekers on what they would have to do to be considered serious contenders for the job. Until then, they had been merely adding descriptions of recent jobs to their already polished résumés. The scores were tabulated and shared at the next meeting. Two candidates stood out as most likely to be invited for the first round of interviews—even though they did not have the most experience or attend the most prestigious schools.

The group discussed why these two résumés, in particular, stood out. The answer was that the two submissions *demonstrated the closest links between what IBM said it was looking for and what was emphasized on the applications, including the résumés.* The exercise encouraged the group members to examine more closely the requirements of each job for which they apply. After the experiment, their résumés became more focused instruments. Shortly thereafter, each member experienced a spike in interviews. Their competitive edge had little to do with the school attended, whom someone knew, or what social group they belonged to. The most important variable was their ability to demonstrate value creation.

Here is an example of changes one person made in her résumé once she focused on value creation:

Current Résumé Section

Director, Executive Staffing, ABC Corporation

‣ Responsible for coordination and direction of executive staffing worldwide (50–60 hires per year).

‣ Successfully met cost/hire and time-to-fill metrics.

‣ Successfully managed professional staff of three recruiters and executive search firms.

Position Description

Company seeks experienced executive staffing professional who will:

‣ Reestablish staffing function credibility as a legitimate business partner.

‣ Facilitate management decision making in a politically sensitive environment.

‣ Meet or exceed strict requirements of cost/hire and time-to-fill standards.

Revised Résumé Section

Director, Executive Staffing, ABC Corporation

‣ Established function's credibility with senior management and other key stakeholders as evidenced by consistent performance rating of outstanding. Shortened new executive learning curve by designing and implementing a year-long orientation/on-boarding program.

‣ Consistently exceeded strict standards of cost/hire (15%) and time to fill (10%). Implemented annual client satisfaction survey as key component of staffing function's continuous improvement effort.

‣ Became respected business partner as evidenced by being asked to join management roundtable (a politically sensitive assignment) to assess new executive contribution as a component of company's annual management review.

The revised résumé section is clearly more focused on the specific requirements of the position, and it promises to create the kind of value the hiring organization is seeking. Another way of looking at value creation is to remember that your résumé is not just a summary of what you have accomplished. It is a promise of what you can accomplish for someone else.

A department head once asked whether it was more important to "look good" or "be good." His answer came as a surprise to the staff. He said, "Look good." His rationale was that if you are, in fact, no good, you will be found out soon enough. But if you do not at least look the part, no one will ever have enough confidence to give you a chance to perform. In this case, "looking the part" means constructing a résumé that speaks specifically to the value a hiring organization is looking to be created.

As it turns out, there is ample opportunity to create value in a variety of settings, including as a traditional or nontraditional employee or as an entrepreneur.

Create Value as a Traditional Employee

In a job market in which more people with college degrees are competing for fewer good jobs, the advantage goes to those who most closely approximate the skills and contributions employers are looking to acquire. Hiring managers prefer people who can make a difference to their bottom line. Your ability to demonstrate that potential by drawing parallels between your previous experiences and an employer's needs is crucial in getting hired and remaining employed.

The ability to demonstrate value creation, thus, is a fundamental requirement of the new job market. It is as simple as putting yourself in the shoes of the employer. In our workshops, we do this by asking the question: Whom do you hire? We answer it by listing two sets of credentials side by side and comparing them to the job specifications from the employer. Workshop participants get it every time. The school you attended and your college major are much less important than your ability to extrapolate what an employer requires from the experiences and training you currently have.

We cover the steps required to write an effective résumé in our workshop. Here, we begin to reveal how to succeed in today's job market. Most job seekers understand that a résumé is a onetime opportunity to establish a link to a potential employer. How do they create a document that puts their best foot forward? The light begins to go on when they understand that *their résumé is not really about them.* In fact, the best résumés—and the ones against which you must compete— are arrows shot directly at their target. They take into account the needs of hiring organizations and then link those needs to the candidate's own accomplishments.

CARESS THE DETAILS

Typical résumés are, more often than not, simply summaries of someone's work history. But those that garner attention do considerably more. That is what Sheila found when she lost her first job, five years out of college. At the time she was working in marketing as a supervisor for a large consumer-products company. She had a run-in with her boss, was fired, and by mutual agreement, they treated it as part of a more general layoff. This happens a lot.

At first, Sheila wasn't too concerned about finding another position because of her solid work experience and her degree from a prestigious university. So, the difficulties she had finding her next job came as a surprise. Sheila discovered that lots of well-educated, out-of-work professionals had her level of experience—and more. It was a mistake to assume that her credentials would "speak for themselves." Eventually, Sheila focused on how her job experiences and education uniquely positioned her to make contributions that were important to the companies to which she applied.

Presenting your credentials to the job market as if your previous work history and college degree are enough to carry the day is a critical mistake. Of necessity, employers are interested, first and foremost, in themselves and their profitability. This applies to not-for-profit sector jobs as well! All organizations want to know what's in it for them if they hire you. Can you create more value than your competition? Remember, many other candidates have the same or similar credentials— you have to demonstrate that your credentials really fit better. You have to make it easy for hiring managers to see how your background will answer their needs. *Always translate your background into what a company needs.*

Never assume that the connection between your experience and the company's needs is obvious—or that the hiring organization will connect the dots. For example, if a company is looking for a financial analyst, it is not enough for it to know that you have been a financial analyst. One client in particular mistakenly thought his résumé should be a summary of "major" areas of responsibility. Meanwhile, the position description specifically called for someone with experience in ad-hoc reporting. Though he had, from time to time, done that kind of work, it was not a major area of his responsibility and so it never made it into his résumé—at least not until it was pointed out that he needed to be more responsive to the needs of the hiring organization, that he needed to create value. The lesson is: Always find out the details of what is required and make sure your résumé includes them. The value the hiring organization is looking to have created is often found in those details.

REALIZE THAT IT'S NOT ABOUT YOU

Initially, our workshop participants are confused when we tell them their résumés are not about them. They wonder if we are suggesting that they lie or exaggerate their accomplishments. The answer is a decided "No!" The résumé describes the truth about what you have to offer, but that truth framed in terms of the hiring organization's needs, not your needs.

Understand that the context for the presentation of your credentials is provided or shaped by the requirements of the position—not vice versa. For example, the way you might position your project-management experience should be driven by the specifics of a company's interest in project management. Even worse, if project management is not a requirement for the position, that credential should not occupy a prominent position as you present your credentials for consideration.

Once their confusion ends about the tail wagging the dog, our clients are better able to present their skills against the backdrop of the job market. It is surprising that so many people put their résumés together without the slightest consideration of what the job market or a particular organization requires. They wonder why they never hear from companies with job openings. For instance, Tom had a Ph.D. in English literature, and he included that as part of the educational summary on his résumé, even though he was looking for an entry-level position in pharmaceutical sales, where he had been working for the past two years.

Tom had applied for a number of advertised positions but was either ignored or advised that he was "overqualified." Companies say that from time to time so as to dismiss candidates in whom they have no interest. They may also be concerned that overqualified applicants will move on to other employment the minute they have a chance. The problem, we decided, was that Tom's résumé was unfocused. It did not provide hiring managers with a compelling reason to consider his candidacy. In a more focused version, the Ph.D. mention was dropped and Tom got two invitations to come in for interviews.

ANTICIPATE THE FUTURE

Once people understand how to create real value for themselves and for their potential employer, two things begin to happen. First, they become more valuable in their current position and less subject to downsizing and outsourcing. At the very least, an organization must do the calculation to determine if it really makes sense to let you go. However, no one should be led astray. Few of us are ever in a position to create enough value to overcome the perceived advantages of mergers and acquisitions, let alone advances in technology. The word *perceived* is used here because the overwhelming number of mergers and acquisitions never return anywhere near their premerger advertised value. That doesn't help you, though.

The second advantage of value creation is not the protection one gets against termination. (Remember, it is still an unstable job market and will remain so for the foreseeable future.) It's that by stressing value creation, you start to realize that you can create a value that is marketable and can be sold to others. That value can be sold either to a single organization through your job search or to multiple organizations that are willing to pay handsomely to get it. Value creation allows you to regain control of your career. Plus, it builds your confidence!

The route you take to sell the value you create will depend on your comfort level and flexibility. The more traditional approach is one of selling your value to a single employer in exchange for security of income and other benefits. But that security is on the wane. At some point, you will have to convince another employer of the value you can create for it as well. In this instance, being fired may not feel any better, but at least you can understand that the problem is not so much with you as it is with an unstable job market.

CARRY OVER THE CONCEPT TO YOUR CHILDREN

If you have children, you know that considerations of the future should include them. You may want to know how to help them with their careers, for example. The job market is so unstable and competitive today that parents are resorting to desperate acts. For example, Christy's parents moved beyond footing the bill for her undergraduate degree and paid $10,000 to have her placed in an unpaid nine-week internship that, in their estimation, would provide her with a competitive edge in the entry-level job market. Though it was a questionable action, they correctly understood that hiring decisions are based on perceptions of the value applicants can create for the companies for which they want to work. An internship (even when paid for by Mom and Dad) can provide that competitive advantage.

The emergence of these kinds of internships as a significant source of access clearly advantages families that are relatively well off, at the expense of others not quite so fortunate. Rather than pay for an unpaid internship, start teaching your children about value creation very early in the game—perhaps as early as middle school. This was the advice my consulting firm gave to the Knowledge Is Power Program (KIPP) as they worked with building the career skills of middle-school kids from underserved communities. Once students leave middle school, they stay tethered to KIPP through a series of employment opportunities and academic support programs all the way through college.

For every job the students took, KIPP would require a one- or two-page essay on what the organization did and what value it created for its clients. The final paragraph or two should focus on their jobs and how they contributed to that value the organization created. The exercises were designed to give students a jump on understanding the link between value creation and hiring. By the time those KIPP students are in college, they will be far ahead of others with regard to understanding what companies look for in entry-level hires.

We know that the number-one concern parents have about their college-age children is whether they will choose a course of study that leads to a stable, well-paying career. Yet, campus recruiters continue to say that the college major is not their number-one priority in hiring. Organizations are more interested in leader-ship qualities and communications and analytical skills. One of the surest ways students can make the leap from college to employment is by understanding the language of value creation and being able to communicate that value potential to hiring companies. It is not so much what the students choose to major in as it is what they learn to do with the knowledge they gain. (See also Appendix A.)

Create Value as a Nontraditional Employee

The contingent workforce is made up of people who have nontraditional work arrangements. Mostly, they are temporary employees and independent contractors who work on an as-needed basis. At one time, outplacement firms advised clients to avoid temporary work because those arrangements got in the way of the search for permanent full-time employment. This advice was given as though contingent work was undesirable. And for some, it is. But the size and complexity of this work-force has grown to approximately 14.8 million workers and is now 11 percent of the U.S. workforce. And according to the *Occupational Outlook Handbook's* projections, it is expected to grow an additional 45 percent. Whether individually desirable or not, nontraditional work arrangements constitute too large an opportunity to dismiss out of hand.

Once people understand their ability to create value, it is a short conceptual leap to considering selling that value to more than one organization at a time. Owning the ability to create value offers you the strength and security of multiple sources of employment. If jobs are here today and gone tomorrow, having multiple sources of income starts to look like a more reliable and less risky path to follow. And it is easy to see how multiple buyers and greater demand than you can reasonably supply can ultimately mean greater income than you would have from a single employer.

For most of us, however, developing multiple sources of income seems an unrealistic idea. That is because we have grown up working for one company at a time, possibly for a long time. Making the leap to the world of contingent work takes courage and imagination. You need to have a skill set that someone wants and the flexibility to deliver your services in a nontraditional setting. The risks involved, both perceived and real, can be daunting.

Are you ready for this new order of jobs? Flexibility is the first quality you need in this field of nontraditional value creation. Perhaps the best indicator of whether you are a candidate is to measure your flexibility. Ask yourself, "Would I prefer to have my current income be salary based and paid at regular intervals, or 100 percent variable and driven by whatever revenue contribution I make to the business, day to day?" If you prefer compensation based on your contribution, you are more willing than most to depart from traditional work arrangements. That's an indicator of your flexibility, a good quality to have in today's job market.

Additionally, nontraditional work is not limited to offering services on an as-needed basis. Even in a single-employer situation, you can use value creation to build a new type of relationship. For instance, Julie grew tired of working for physicians who did not respect her skills as a nurse practitioner. (This, by the way, is by far the most common complaint of nursing professionals.) She had a loyal following of 600 patients, many of whom had demonstrated a willingness to follow her from one practice to another in her never-ending search for a better employer. She finally sent a letter to a new physician group with an offer they couldn't refuse. They found it attractive enough to ask for more information.

"I propose," Julie said, "that I work with you to build a successful practice. I have been in the area for fifteen years and have a loyal cadre of patients who will follow me to this practice." By the end of her interview, the doctors could no longer contain their enthusiasm. They offered her a position at an attractive salary on the spot. Rather than turn it down, she made a counteroffer of a bonus for each new patient she recruited to the practice. In other words, she wanted to work *with*, not *for* the doctors and reap more of the benefits of the value she was creating. Thus, her compensation was based on a nontraditional work arrangement. Julie understood value creation and was willing to assume the risk that came with offering that value in a nontraditional way.

TEMPORARY WORK

Temporary spikes in the demand for people are often met by temporary workers (quasi-employees), sometimes hired through temp agencies. These temporary employees can easily be let go once demand subsides, so organizations prefer them when future demand is uncertain. At one time, temps were largely clerical employees.

Now they include lawyers, accountants, physicians, hospital administrators, sales-persons, executives, and miscellaneous other professionals. Those who are the best at what they do—that is, who create obvious value for the organizations with which they work "temporarily"—are sometimes asked to join on a permanent, full-time basis. In this sense, the temporary work is a trial run, during which both organization and employee get to know one another. Today's temporary workers can also command substantial compensation by selling their skills to the highest bidder or to multiple bidders. In short, the old advice to avoid temporary employment is not as reliable as it once was.

Temporary positions can have benefits that serve both parties. Robert, a physician friend, leaped at the chance to become the "temporary" CEO of a medium-size hospital chain. The opportunity was attractive to Robert because it allowed him to commute rather than relocate. It was attractive to the hospital because having a "temp" in the position gave the hospital board time to make a more deliberate decision. The arrangement lasted a little over two years—the length of time it took to groom an internal candidate who was not fully ready when the opening first occurred.

The temporary employee who tracks the contribution (value) he or she creates, and who broadcasts those experiences to others who also may need those services, is uniquely positioned to capture the dynamism of today's job market. Risky? Perhaps—but no more so than relying on a traditional job in a company more interested in return on shareholder equity than on your personal well-being. As our society transitions from one workforce configuration to another, the opportunity to remain employed on a temporary basis grows as well.

AS-NEEDED CONTINGENCY WORK

Once Leigh understood value creation, she started her curriculum-design business. Companies with small training departments that want to offer an in-house curriculum often choose to hire outside consultants to design those programs. Leigh has been in the business for seven years, and as her clients move to other companies in the metropolitan area and beyond, they use her curriculum-design services as needed, on a contingent basis. All of her brand development and advertising is word of mouth, and she works hours that allow for an active social life and for raising three children.

People are often surprised to learn that Leigh does not have a graduate degree, because she runs a successful business in a field that usually requires one. "How do you respond," she was once asked, "when a request for proposal (RFP) calls for a master's degree?"

"I ignore it, list my references, and apply for the work anyway. And I get a lot of it." Her reputation for solid work trumps the degree requirement every time. That would likely not be the case if companies were considering her for full-time work. She had initially developed her curriculum-design skills as a clerical employee who took advantage of internal-development programs and on-the-job training. Once her department was downsized, Leigh found a niche in the job market that would likely not be there in a more traditional setting.

Although value creation can be applied across a wide spectrum of situations, it is of particular use in the world of white-collar work, and it is crucial to any attempts to offer as-needed services. Experienced workers, tossed about by job instability, can summon their knowledge and skills to offer that value as services on an as-needed basis, thereby working more for themselves than for others.

Create Value for Yourself as an Entrepreneur

While the age of entrepreneurial innovation is upon us, it is not for the faint of heart. Starting your own business can be a high-risk/high-reward game, with implications that may not be fully understood at the start. No less prominent a figure than Warren Buffett counseled against this game's excesses when he noted that all great opportunities include innovators, imitators, and idiots.[1] Figuring out where you stand in the lineup is no easy task. Innovators make a contribution to society, but they do not necessarily make money because they often have to focus on running the operation that turns their ideas into practical products or services. Early imitators often make money because the ideas they have copied are new, still in demand, and operationally functional. In this sense, it is often better to be a trend-spotter than a trendsetter. The idiots, of course, are the "too little, too late" participants who try to cash in on an opportunity well past its peak.

The gourmet coffeehouse craze, prompted by the initial success of Starbucks and copied by numerous others, is a case in point. Rather than meeting an insatiable demand, new entrants now find the business tough sledding. This business sector may be a contracting market, with dramatically smaller profit margins than just a few years ago.

Innovation will also continue to appear, however, and it makes sense to be on the lookout for opportunities wherever you can find them. Who knew, for example, that ordinary people could safely lend money to strangers at a return below what banks and credit card companies charge, but well above what they can earn elsewhere? That idea started as a trickle on the eBay copycat www.prosper.com and quickly grew into a multibillion-dollar business with thousands of participants. Making a living from innovation requires both nontraditional thinking and a tolerance for risk.

Entrepreneurial innovation has been a particular boon for women, especially returning moms. What happened to Tina is a case in point. She met Dave while in college, they got married, and they decided to get his career up and running first and then she would soon follow suit. Three children and one divorce later, Tina was trying to kick-start her career. The difference now was that she really needed the money but didn't have the support or experience to command the salary required to maintain her standard of living. The demands of a tight job market posed a unique set of problems for Tina and legions of other women like her.

Tina was eventually able to distinguish herself from the competition (that is, she was able to create value) because she learned how to cobble together experiences that emphasized her unique ability to multitask, organize, and attend to details. She first landed a job as a personal assistant for a busy executive who worked for a local nonprofit agency. This experience and the same skill set led her to develop a successful concierge service for busy women executives—especially those with young children.

Thus, a variety of people are finding their niches in the new job world as entrepreneurs. These groups include returning veterans, stay-at-home moms, newly graduating college students, laid-off white-collar workers, and many others. The current reduced barriers to entry and the ability to develop scale without cost have put even global business ownership within reach of many of us. The most risky of the three options for creating value, entrepreneurship can be the most personally rewarding.

❯ ❯ ❯

By now you have a good understanding of what it takes to be successful in today's job market: the concept value creation. That understanding now needs to be converted into specific action steps. That is, you need to focus on the mechanics of value creation, which begins with discussion of Rule #2. It is here where value creation really begins to come to life.

> **• • • • • • • • • • Things to Remember • • • • • • • • •**
>
> ▶ *If you are feeling bad about not being able to hold on to or find white-collar work, there is nothing wrong with you, and you should know it. The job market has changed and it lacks the stability many people are seeking.*
>
> ▶ *The major sources of workforce instability continue to be globalization, advances in technology, and deregulation. Jobs move from one place to another almost at will, which has created new rules for finding white-collar work.*
>
> ▶ *Today's workforce can be divided into three sectors, depending on the type of employment agreement each has: traditional, nontraditional, and entrepreneurial. There are numerous opportunities for career survival and prosperity in each sector for those who understand the language of value creation.*
>
> ▶ *All of us will have to learn to create value for ourselves and others. Because the job market is overcrowded, allowing our credentials to "speak for themselves" is no longer sufficient. Job and career opportunities go disproportionately to those who learn to focus on the value others want us to create. Value creation has become a competitive edge.*

NOTE

1. "Charlie Rose Interviews Warren Buffett," PBS, Wednesday, October 1, 2008.

RULE #2

Your Résumé: It's About the Value You Create

TURBULENT TIMES like today, when there are new rules for finding white-collar work, create opportunities to apply new principles that can set you apart from the job-seeking pack. You do that throughout the job-application process, and the first step is to develop a value-infused résumé.

To start, you need to grasp two important concepts. The first is that value is in the eye of the beholder. And that "eye" is the eyes of those making the hiring decisions. They have defined what is of value to them and will base their choice on their estimation of who best provides the value they seek. As the stakes have risen, decision makers can no longer afford to simply hire friends and relatives, without giving consideration for the comparative value of other candidates. Nor can they remain in the cocoon of the status quo, doing things the way they were done before. In a globally competitive economy, value-added potential is often more important for job seekers than formal credentials.

Second, this value is not about you. We have fallen into the habit of putting our credentials forward as if they have intrinsic value for anyone to see. A college degree is a case in point. The value of a college degree depends on what the hiring organization assigns it. It is in this sense that the job marketplace is about what others need from us. The most effective job seeker recognizes a company's need and tries to deliver it in a competitive environment.

Value creation is not a simpleminded pandering to the wishes of others. It is a way to get in touch with a marketplace increasingly dominated by technology and globalization—one in which the customer is king and personal brand is a critical component of how to reach that customer. And customers evaluate companies on their ability to deliver value. So it follows that companies evaluate potential employees on their perceptions of those employees' ability to help with the value they seek to create.

Without a concentrated focus on value creation, you are less likely to land the job you want. You need to understand the specifics of how value creation really works and use them to develop your résumé—the first door to your new job.

How to Fill Your Résumé with Value

In our workshops on résumé writing, we clarify how value creation really works. We ask workshop participants to think about how they should put their résumés together and then share their thoughts with the class. Before reading ahead, ask yourself the same question. Think of facing blank sheets of paper—ones that will eventually be turned into your résumé. How will you go about it?

The most common approach (even after people hear their résumés are not about them) is to start with your previous work history or education. As instructors, we know that people understand the concepts but do not have the tools to apply them. As a result, they tend to start where they always have—with themselves and with what they have accomplished. To get them to start elsewhere—namely, with the hiring organization—we came up with a new exercise. We call it the "Personalization of Value" and use it in all our workshops.

Each group is asked to take a few minutes to write a couple of sentences on what value means to them and share it with the rest of the group. The answers vary a great deal. All, however, have one thing in common—they are things individuals define for themselves. Value to them is "their" value. Then, we explain that we could have easily made an educated guess about what value means to them without asking them and would have produced a close approximation of what they eventually told us. But it would not have been as accurate as asking for their participation. It is a short conceptual leap to show that hiring managers and the companies they represent behave much the same way as individuals. That is, they define value for themselves—just as most individuals do.

However, when you're sending out your résumé, value is not about you. We don't mean that the values and skills candidates bring to the hiring situation are unimportant. You just have to put yourself in the company's shoes. Organizations are looking to exchange their resources for your contribution—where they have a sense of what they need, in what quantity they need it, and how much they are willing to pay. Your success in landing the job depends on your ability to find out what it is that they value, and deliver it to them in your initial application for the position.

At this point, workshop participants begin to get it, but they do not have enough tools to apply the concept to their résumés. They also do not have the requisite mindset. Any time you prepare a résumé and apply for a position without fully understanding what is of value to the hiring organization, the application will likely reflect what is important to you and be little more than an educated guess about what is important to it. My friends in the employment business tell me that far too many of the résumés they see fall into this category. The contrast between these and other résumés focused on the problems an organization is trying to solve is too great to ignore. Focused documents stand out and get most of the attention.

Applicants sometimes wonder why they submit résumés for jobs for which they see themselves as a perfect fit but they never get as much as an e-mail acknowledgment that they applied. More often than not, their submission reflects what is of importance to them. Simply put, an educated guess about what is of importance to the hiring organization is not enough.

Instead, you find out what the hiring organization values by carefully reading the position description for the job in which you are interested. You also review the company's website and industry publications. These three sources will help you identify the key words the company uses to communicate what they want.

Five Steps to Your Value-Infused Résumé

Putting a résumé together is not easy. That's one of the reasons templates are so popular. Rather than forcing you to think about what needs to be said, templates direct you to the correct format and some of its content. You do end up with a professional-looking document, but little more. This one-size-fits-all approach has several disadvantages, including that your résumé looks like thousands of other unfocused documents and none of them will likely appeal to the hiring manager who interviews. This has become such a big problem that companies with open positions often hire personnel just to wade through the pile of résumés that invariably accompany a posting for a white-collar position. It also explains why seasoned HR pros spend little more than fifteen seconds reviewing each initial submission. The overwhelming majority are generic documents that provide little relevant information.

Creating a focused, value-filled résumé will help you break through the clutter. You can still use a template. In fact, for purposes of format, we recommend that you use Microsoft Word templates. Our materials, though, focus on content rather than format. While we do provide format guidelines, other formats can be used just as effectively as long as you emphasize the value you bring to a particular situation.

So, how do you find out what companies value? As mentioned, you *read the position description for the job in which you are interested, visit the company's website,* and *review the industry publications.* Companies go to great lengths to tell you what they value. You just have to know where to look. To understand more precisely what they are saying, you can use our "Key Word" exercise tool. We have included an actual job description for a middle-management position in the financial services industry for you to follow as we go through the steps required to build a value-infused résumé. The same rules apply when you develop a résumé for other positions, regardless of industry and whether the hiring institution is in a public, private, or not-for-profit organization.

STEP 1: IDENTIFY THE EMPLOYER'S KEY WORDS

The first step in the process is to locate a position description and highlight all of the key words. Key words clarify the skills an employer is looking for in a new hire. They also identify issues a company is currently facing and provide insight into the role the position plays in the organization. Highlight all the action verbs, adjectives, and skills that refer to the attributes the employer is looking for in an ideal candidate. These, then, are the skills of most importance to the employer and they represent the value it seeks in the person who will fill the position. This is critically important because you will use these words throughout the application process. In particular, employers will likely spot these words when they give your résumé an initial look. Therefore, including them in the body of your résumé will help distinguish you from other candidates. See Figure 2.1 for an example of a highlighted position from ACME Bank.

FIGURE 2.1 Highlighted position description.

Director, Financial Planning and Analysis

ACME BANK

ACME Bank is an integrated financial service organization providing personal, business, corporate, and institutional clients with banking, lending, investing, and financial management solutions. We are deeply committed to a high-performance culture, one that values diversity, continuous learning, employee commitment, and community involvement.

We reward our talented professionals with a base salary and competitive compensation package, life, health, dental, pension plan, 401(k), and an exceptional working environment.

SPECIFIC ACCOUNTABILITIES

Strategy

▶ Understand the corporate initiatives of the Bank, participate in or develop future-oriented strategies to maximize shareholder value as required

▶ Partner with clients to develop future-oriented strategies to maximize shareholder value.

Advisory

▶ Provide consulting and support to customers by continually offering value-added ideas, advice, and solutions.

▶ Work in partnership with the client to assist in optimal structuring of new initiatives and strategies. Ensure that structures comply with regulatory rules and guidelines.

▶ Work as a valued business partner to develop, implement, and track value-maximizing strategies—business planning, forecasting, and reporting on results.

▶ Provide financial advice to clients on impacts of various business transactions (investments/divestitures, securitizations, etc).

Governance and Analysis/Results

▶ Provide weekly, monthly, quarterly, and annual reports as required.

▶ Prepare both formal and informal reports and analysis for the client as required to support strategic objectives, decision making, and solution resolution.

(continued)

▶ Be responsible for ensuring that risks are identified and mitigated.

▶ Coordinate the annual planning processes.

▶ Review and provide financial concurrence related to the approval of a capital expenditure.

▶ Attest as required to LOB's compliance with applicable policies, including corporate policies and accounting policies. Provide input and concurrence to new policies impacting LOB.

Support

▶ Lead or participate in project teams as required for new initiatives, process improvements, or technology implementation and development.

▶ Provide leadership by recruiting, developing, and maintaining high-quality staff, and ensuring that processes are in place to do this.

▶ Responsible for staff training and development.

▶ Responsible for providing ongoing feedback on performance and ensuring timely completion of annual review process.

▶ Ensure that skill levels remain commensurate with the requirements of the position.

▶ Responsible for identifying skills gaps and taking appropriate actions to close those gaps.

▶ Key Contacts: LOB and Group executives, Controllers Bank of Montreal Group of Companies, Finance departments.

▶ Internal/external auditors, Regulatory agencies VBM

▶ Support VBM initiatives by understanding VBM metrics, providing financial information, and performing VBM-based analysis as required.

Knowledge & Skills

▶ CPA or degree in Accounting/Finance

▶ 6–8 years of work experience in a financial services environment

▶ Knowledge of banking structures

▶ Strong interpersonal, verbal, and written communication skills

▶ Experience in preparing and delivering presentations

▶ Experience in planning, forecasting, and analysis

▶ Project, process, and change management skills

▶ Good working knowledge of LAN-based software programs including Word, Excel, PowerPoint

To explore this opportunity to join ACME Bank, visit our website and apply for position Job ID 55555 at www.acmebank.com.

Notice the words in the example that we chose not to highlight. Some examples include "high-performance culture," "formal and informal reports," and "technology implementation." In our judgment, these were less important than the words we highlighted. Use your best judgment when reviewing other position descriptions. The more you practice, the better you will get at it.

Then visit the company's website and note the verbs, adjectives, and skills that refer to key values at the company. This provides insight into its culture and reflects what it thinks are important attributes for employees in general. Do the same thing as you read through industry publications and use the key words there, especially if you cannot find an appropriate position description. As you conduct your job search, note common terms from one company to the next that represent value industry-wide. You will have to tweak your résumé less as you apply for similar jobs in different companies. See Figure 2.2 for an excerpt from ACME Bank's website.

FIGURE 2.2 Excerpt from ACME Bank website.

ACME BANK VALUES

ACME Bank draws upon a set of well-articulated values to create long-term, sustainable results. These values ensure strong relationships with clients—and outstanding opportunities for our experienced professionals to meet their personal and career goals. At Acme Bank, we live the following values each and every day:

Client Focus
We put our clients first.

Honesty and Integrity
We expect it of ourselves, of each other, and in our dealings with our clients.

Creating Value
We are committed to creating value and wealth for our clients, which, in turn, creates value for our employees and our shareholders.

Respect
Our respect for one another and our clients is evident in all our interactions.

Diversity
We strive to create a workplace that is inclusive of all.

Now, compile a list of those key words that you highlighted and organize them by category. Place an asterisk next to key words mentioned more than once or that you think are particularly important. As you put the final version of your résumé together, you will want to give these words a second look, and make sure you use them in an appropriate context.

The key words from the sample job description and website have been placed into categories (see Figure 2.3) for easy reference. Notice that this particular job description categorized the job requirements, so we brought these categories into our list of key words. Also, notice where we placed asterisks and make sure you understand why they are there. We have found the categories used here to apply to any résumé, but it is okay to come up with your own.

FIGURE 2.3 Key words by category.

Strategy	Advisory	Governance and Analysis/Results	Support	Knowledge & Skills
*Develop future-oriented strategies	Consulting and support customers	Timely reports	Lead or participate in project teams	*Creating value
*Maximize shareholder value	Offer value-added ideas, advice, and solutions	Risk identification and mitigation	Lead and recruit staff	CPA or Accounting/Finance degree
Partner with clients/client focus	New initiatives	Coordinate	Train staff	6–8 years of experience
	Implement and track business planning, forecasting, and reporting on results	Provide financial concurrence	Performance feedback	Knowledge of banking structures
		Review capital expenditures	Skills gap identification	Strong interpersonal, verbal, and written communication skills
	Advise on investments/divestitures, and securitizations	LOB's compliance	LOB and Group executive relationships	Prepare and deliver presentations
			VBM metrics	Planning, forecasting, analysis
			VBM-based analysis	Project, process, and change management skills

STEP 2: LIST YOUR EXPERIENCES

You are ready to begin setting the focus on your background. These experiences are important, but the output from this step is not your résumé. This is where many people start and end as they prepare their résumé. As you will see, many stop short of infusing their experiences with value. And too often, that approach results in an unfocused résumé that is not tied to the value an employer is asking to have created. No wonder these résumés miss their mark. Most are written without taking the interests of the employer into account.

Take a look at Figure 2.4 as an example of what your list of experiences should look like. As you draw it up, make sure:

▶ It is in reverse chronological order—that is, the most recent experiences are listed first.

▶ You state the job title and task performed in each job.

▶ You recall as many relevant details as possible, such as your responsibilities and accomplishments.

FIGURE 2.4 List of experiences.

Employer	Dates	Position	Experiences
Big Service Firm	2002–2004	Director of Finance, US Commercial Operations	▸ Proposed and led the development of the revenue planning tool. ▸ Led negotiations that enabled the launch of a restructured US commercial organization. ▸ Converted a group of financial technicians into a high-performance global resource.
Acme Marketing Company	1999–2002	Director, Global Business Analysis	▸ Designed and implemented the new client revenue forecasting model and financial planning package across the company. ▸ Researched, analyzed, and presented all P&L and balance sheet forecasts with projections and calculations associated with acquisitions. ▸ Created and produced the company's first comprehensive global strategic plan.
Big Drug Company 1988–1999	1998–1999	Manager, Competitive Analysis and Forecasting, Medical Products Marketing	▸ Directed the commercial analysis and forecasting for the new development business units and provided the competitive analysis activities for all business units in this division. ▸ Developed the analysis and negotiated the proposal that led to a strategic alliance agreement between the company and an outside pharmaceutical company. ▸ Created an in-depth analysis of a major therapeutic category and developed the proper launch positioning and resources that supported the product being licensed to launch in the US.

(continued)

Employer	Dates	Position	Experiences
Big Drug Company 1988–1999	1996–1997	Associate Manager, Micromarketing, Medical Products Marketing	• Directed staff in physician targeting and analysis for the marketing and sales organizations. • Refocused the Internet promotion on spending. • Reengineered the promotions analysis process and vendor relationships. • Integrated promotions planning tools into the market planning process.
Big Drug Company 1988–1999	1988–1995	Early Management	• Managed teams. • Provided financial leadership on the multifunctional strategic team for the division's major product line. • Developed the strategic project model that was adopted by all commercial teams in the Hospital Care Division. • Researched, analyzed, and created financial pricing and P&L proposals for all the major hospital buying group contracts. • Developed and produced commercial sales and profit forecasts for the electronic drug delivery product line.

You probably won't use every experience on the list. That's okay. Past experiences that are not relevant for this job may be useful when applying for others.

STEP 3: INFUSE YOUR EXPERIENCE WITH VALUE

When you quantify and qualify each of your experiences, you infuse them with value, especially when you insert words and phrases identified in the "Key Word" exercise. This is an important part of the process—one that grows easier as you get the hang of it. Stay with it and be diligent. Make note in the example (see Figure 2.5) of the source we identify for each insertion.

Here is what you do. Revisit each accomplishment statement and ask, "How did I create value for this accomplishment?" Value, in this sense, has three aspects—results that can be either quantified or qualified and/or that include language an employer uses to express value.

Quantitative Results. The most obvious quantitative results include numerical indicators such as dollar figures. They are universally understood and equated with value regardless of industry or type of organization.

FIGURE 2.5 Examples of accomplishment statements.

Employer	Dates	Position	Accomplishment Statements
Big Service Firm	2002–2004	Director of Finance, US Commercial Operations	‣ Proposed and led the development of the revenue planning tool *that increased sales force and finance team productivity 65 percent while increasing revenue forecasting accuracy, then organized and managed the consultant team that implemented the project.* Received the 2002 Award for Excellence for this effort. ‣ Led negotiations for *data acquisition, licensing agreements, joint ventures, and organizational restructuring* that enabled the launch of a restructured US commercial organization *with optimal initiatives and strategies.* ‣ Converted a group of diversified financial technicians using value-maximizing strategies into a high-performance global resource by setting high expectations for the department, training them in sophisticated new skills, and coaching each one on communication and presentation techniques.
Acme Marketing Company	1999–2002	Director, Global Business Analysis	‣ *Partnered with clients* to design and implement the new client revenue forecasting model and financial planning package across the company, *greatly improving the management team's ability to efficiently and effectively manage financial performance.* ‣ Researched, analyzed, and presented all P&L and balance sheet forecasts in clear, concise form, projecting changes in revenue, operating income, debt levels, cash position, interest payments, and compensation calculations associated with acquisitions. ‣ Created and produced the company's first comprehensive global strategic plan by *reengineering the process, standardizing the formats and reports, and leading the reviews with senior management and the executive board.*
Big Drug Company 1988–1999	1998–1999	Manager, Competitive Analysis and Forecasting, Medical Products Marketing	‣ Directed the commercial analysis and forecasting for the new development business units with annual sales exceeding $1 billion, while providing the competitive analysis activities for all business units in this $4 billion division. ‣ Analyzed corporate initiatives and negotiated the proposal that led to a $50 million strategic alliance agreement between the company and an outside pharmaceutical company.

(continued)

Employer	Dates	Position	Accomplishment Statements
			‣ Created an in-depth analysis of a major therapeutic category and coordinated the proper launch positioning and resources that supported the product being licensed to launch in the US. The 2002 revenues for this product exceeded $400 million. ‣ Directed external consultant teams in developing actionable analyses on market and competitive developments by offering value-added ideas, advice, and solutions.
Big Drug Company 1988–1999	1996–1997	Associate Manager, Micromarketing, Medical Products Marketing	‣ Directed staff of eight financial and marketing professionals in physician targeting and analysis for the marketing and sales organizations with an emphasis on ROI for the $100 million promotions budget. ‣ Refocused the Internet promotion spending, improving communication to target audiences and saving $700,000 annually. ‣ Reengineered the promotions analysis process and vendor relationships, which cut the time of analysis turnaround from four weeks to one week while reducing analysis costs 70 percent. ‣ Integrated promotions planning tools into the market planning process, which provided high visibility of costs and maximized promotion spending ROI.
Big Drug Company 1988–1999	1988–1995	Early Management	‣ *Managed teams using continuous learning techniques in several diverse operating divisions.* ‣ Provided *financial leadership* on the multifunctional strategic team for the division's major product line. The team projects achieved annual cost reduction savings exceeding $3 million. ‣ Developed the strategic project model that was adopted by all commercial teams in the $1.5 billion Hospital Care Division that *streamlined investment decision making.* ‣ Researched, analyzed, and created financial pricing and P&L proposals to ensure risks were identified and mitigated for all the major hospital buying group contracts. ‣ Developed and *produced highly analytical* commercial sales and profit forecasts for the $100 million electronic drug delivery product line.

Qualitative Results. It isn't always possible to express accomplishments in exact amounts. Qualitative results are often just as useful and include phrases like, "first place," "top rank," or "1 out of xx."

Value Language. The key words and language you got from an employer's position description, website, or industry publications represent expressions of value and are language the employer will recognize.

In Figure 2.5, you see rewritten accomplishment statements with quantitative and qualitative value infused in them. Though key words are used throughout the list, pay particular attention to those that are italicized and in bold type. They are perhaps the most obvious examples from the exercise. Obvious examples of quantification and qualification show up when the words are italicized only. To get the full effect of this step, compare the accomplishment statements here with those from the previous example in Step 2. Your accomplishment statements should show a similar contrast.

STEP 4: SELECT THE BEST STATEMENTS

The purpose of this step is to choose the best statements for your résumé. Again, focus on what is important to the employer/industry where you want to work. Once you have created the list of the value-infused accomplishment statements, select and rank in order the best five or six statements according to the following criteria:

▶ Does this statement illustrate specific value I have created?

▶ Is the value I have created useful to my prospective employer? How?

If you can answer affirmatively both questions, then include the accomplishment statement on your résumé. If you cannot answer yes to both questions, then do not include it on your résumé. If you are unsure if the statement creates value, chances are the hiring manager will not be able to recognize it either, so leave it off. Be aware that there will likely be other accomplishment statements that do not bear directly on what this employer is looking for. Set these aside for now and make sure only those with direct bearing for this job are included in your résumé.

Add the others only as space permits. Remember, while these may be important to you, they may not be important to the employer. You may use different accomplishment statements for different versions of your résumé. See Figure 2.6 for our example's list of value-infused accomplishment statements.

STEP 5: FORMAT AND REFINE YOUR RÉSUMÉ

You are close to assembling the final product. Let's spend a few moments to format and refine what you have already accomplished. Remember: feel free to use other formats. By and large, one is just as good as another. We know from experience that companies are more interested in content than they are in format. What is important is that the value you bring to a particular situation is clear and emphasized.

There are two basic types of résumés: reverse chronological and functional. Our focus is on the reverse chronological type because it is the most commonly used. It groups your work experiences in reverse chronological order—that is, from the most recent experience to your very first relevant job.

In general, functional résumés create suspicion because readers often think applicants are trying to hide something, especially long periods of unemployment. In a functional résumé, work experience is grouped according to the type of work performed. There are three types of people who should consider using a functional résumé: a person changing careers, a person returning to work after a substantial break (returning mothers), and independent consultants. A functional résumé can highlight each type of work that relates to the job description. An example of a functional résumé has been included for reference (Appendix D).

For the next few pages, we will detail the different sections of a chronological résumé and walk through the process for constructing each one. There are four basic sections of a résumé:

1. Header

2. Summary

3. Professional Experience (this is where the refinement takes place)

4. Background

FIGURE 2.6 Selected value-infused accomplishment statements.

PROFESSIONAL EXPERIENCES

▶ Proposed and led the development of the revenue planning tool that increased sales force and finance team productivity 65 percent while increasing revenue forecasting accuracy, then organized and managed the consultant team that implemented the project. Received the 2002 Award for Excellence for this effort.

▶ Led negotiations for data acquisition, licensing agreements, joint ventures, and organizational restructuring that enabled the launch of a restructured US commercial organization with optimal initiatives and strategies.

▶ Converted a group of diversified financial technicians using value-maximizing strategies into a high-performance global resource by setting high expectations for the department, training them in sophisticated new skills, and coaching each one on communication and presentation techniques.

▶ Partnered with clients to design and implement the new client revenue forecasting model and financial planning package across the company, greatly improving the management team's ability to efficiently and effectively manage financial performance.

▶ Researched, analyzed, and presented all P&L and balance sheet forecasts in clear, concise form, projecting changes in revenue, operating income, debt levels, cash position, interest payments, and compensation calculations associated with acquisitions.

▶ Created and produced the company's first comprehensive global strategic plan by reengineering the process, standardizing the formats and reports, and leading the reviews with senior management and the executive board.

▶ Analyzed corporate initiatives and negotiated the proposal that led to a $50 million strategic alliance agreement between the company and an outside pharmaceutical company.

▶ Created an in-depth analysis of a major therapeutic category and coordinated the proper launch positioning and resources that supported the product being licensed to launch in the US. The 2002 revenues for this product exceeded $400 million.

▶ Directed external consultant teams in developing actionable analyses on market and competitive developments by offering value-added ideas, advice, and solutions.

▶ Refocused the Internet promotion spending, improving communication to target audiences and saving $700,000 annually.

▶ Reengineered the promotions analysis process and vendor relationships, which cut the time of analysis turnaround from four weeks to one week while reducing analysis costs 70 percent.

▶ Integrated promotions planning tools into the market planning process, which provided high visibility of costs and maximized promotion spending ROI.

▶ Provided financial leadership on the multifunctional strategic team for the division's major product line. The team projects achieved annual cost reduction savings exceeding $3 million.

▶ Developed the strategic project model that was adopted by all commercial teams in the $1.5 billion Hospital Care Division that streamlined investment decision making.

▶ Developed and produced highly analytical commercial sales and profit forecasts for the $100 million electronic drug delivery product line.

Header

The first-page header includes:

- Name
- Home address
- Phone number(s)
- E-mail address

General guidelines for constructing a header include commonsense suggestions: do not use more than two phone numbers (home and cell) and use a professional e-mail name. Do not use something you consider funny or cute. If you need to create a temporary, separate e-mail account during your job search, do so, but be diligent in checking it.

Below is an example of a first page header and is applicable for middle- and senior-level positions. Center the header at the top of the page:

> **MICHELLE STREET**
> 9501 Any Street
> Chicago, IL 60600
> Michelle@buzztech.com

The second-page header need only be your name on the extreme left and page number on the right. Below is an example of a second-page header.

> MICHELLE STREET   Page 2

Summary

The summary section includes three or four statements that describe your current and future goals. It is not a career history. It typically includes four statements broken down as follows:

STATEMENT 1—BRAND STATEMENT

Your Brand Statement describes what you are known for or what you want to be known for in your targeted industry.

Guidelines for Writing Your Brand Statement

▶ Indicate your function or industry label.

▶ Indicate your position in the organizational hierarchy. This is accomplished with the very first words of your brand statement as indicated below:

– *Professional* means "not in management."

– *Management professional* means "middle manager."

– *Executive* means head of function in corporate or division, very senior staff, chief officer, or consultant to senior management.

– *Senior leader* is an option for those who do not want to use "management professional" or "executive."

▶ Do not begin the sentence with "I am a . . ." Instead, begin with your function or industry label and vertical definition. For example: "Senior management financial professional with a proven record of . . ."

▶ If desired, use an introductory adjective such as *advanced* before the function or industry label and vertical definition. The higher your level, the less likely you should use the adjective.

Following is an example of a Brand Statement:

Senior management financial professional with a proven record of developing future-oriented strategies that maximize shareholder value.

You should be able to tell that this résumé was submitted by someone in middle management. Now is a good time to reread the definitions and make sure you understand why.

STATEMENT 2—BACKGROUND OR EXPERIENCE STATEMENT

▶ Your background or experience statement indicates your key areas of required experience for the target type of position.

▶ This statement should match the key areas of business for the company or industry.

▶ The sentence begins with, "Background includes . . ." or, "Key areas of experience include . . ."

For example:

Background includes financial management, strategic planning, marketing, and business development.

STATEMENTS 3 AND 4—KEY ATTRIBUTE STATEMENTS

▶ State your strengths and motivated abilities linked to typical outcomes.

▶ Map these statements to the company's mission statement, website, or job description.

▶ Express a sense of your personality.

For example:

A creative thinker who can bring an innovative approach to difficult business issues: An energetic and enthusiastic leader with a reputation for developing strong partner relationships and interfacing with all levels of organizations.

Please note we recommend the "summary" over an "objective statement" because the objective statement only tells an employer what you want to do, not what you are known for.

The following is an example of all four statements together to create the Summary section:

Senior management financial professional with a proven track record of developing future-oriented strategies that maximize shareholder value:

Background includes financial management, strategic planning, marketing, and business development: A creative thinker who can bring an innovative approach to difficult business issues: An energetic and enthusiastic leader with a reputation for developing strong partner relationships and interfacing with all levels of organizations.

Professional Experience

The work you have done to this point provides an excellent foundation for the refinement that comes next. At this point, you have established your format and now you are ready to insert and further refine your accomplishment statements.

In this section, again list your professional experience in reverse chronological order with the most recent jobs or experiences first. Typically, you list all of your past experience since graduating college. However, if you have an extensive work history, you may use synopsis statements to summarize early work history along with the dates.

To begin, list all of the places you have worked. You will use the accomplishment statements from Figure 2.6. Guidelines for each component of the Professional Experience section of the résumé are listed in Figure 2.7. Once you have reviewed them, we will discuss additional tweaking that may be necessary.

RESULTS–ACTION FORMAT

We have not mentioned it before, but now is a good time to be more precise about the structure of the accomplishment statements. Each one should include a result and an action. You start the statement with the result because it is easier to write and it catches the reader's attention. The result should be phrased in terms of typical performance criteria of the job where you realized the accomplishment.

For example, not every job impacts the business measures, but every job has performance measures. Often the performance criteria consist of meeting or exceeding a standard of performance. Meeting or exceeding that standard over an extended period of time, like years, is a major accomplishment.

The *action* shows the skill set you used to get things done. There are two key parts to your skill set: the ability you used and the knowledge involved. Make sure that you use plenty of verbs and that those verbs are related to your abilities. You

FIGURE 2.7 Guidelines for professional experiences section of your résumé.

Component	Description	Guidelines
Company Information	Company, Name, City, State and years of your employment.	‣ You do not have to break down the years of employment into months, unless you want to.
Company Description	Define the business performed by the company.	‣ Pull the description from the company's website and condense it for your needs. ‣ Try to include quantifying facts, such as revenue, net income, number of clients, or number of locations.
Job Title/Position	Define the scope of the stated position underneath it using one or two sentences.	‣ Concentrate on defining the dimension and challenges, not the duties. ‣ Differentiate each position and show progression of your work experience. ‣ Think through each position and realize why that job was important to the organization. ‣ Remember—your résumé is most valuable to you. It can help you talk about your value.
Accomplishments	Explain how well you performed the job listed using bullet points and a result-action format.	‣ Include any awards as a second sentence under the accomplishment for which it was won. ‣ Limit bullet points generally to no longer than two sentences and not exceeding four lines of text. ‣ Use strong adjectives, adverbs, and action verbs.

may be able to qualify and/or quantify actions as well. As you think about the action taken, also include special conditions that may have made your accomplishments even more noticeable. For example, consider the following:

‣ *Circumstances.* Was there anything about the situation that made it difficult to get things done (limited time, short-handed, occurred during a reorganization, etc.)? This is usually expressed as a phrase. It can relate to either the results or the actions.

‣ *Complexity/Sensitivity.* Were there things you worked on or actions you took that were complicated or sensitive? This will usually be expressed as a modifier word, adjective, or adverb. Examples for actions: *carefully, clearly, simultaneously, frequently.*

‣ *Amount of Work.* Did it take a lot of work to complete the accomplishment? Pay particular attention to the skills and abilities you used to make yourself successful. This will usually be expressed as verbs in the action portion of the statement. The verbs will give your writing energy and action orientation. The more verbs you use, the more work it looks like you did—obviously within reason.

USE GOOD, BETTER, BEST

The following illustrates how to take an accomplishment statement from "good" to "better" to "best" by quantifying the results and detailing the difficulty level. Here is an example of a *good* accomplishment statement:

> Developed and implemented a new order-entry system.

You can turn it into a *better* accomplishment statement by quantifying the results. Ask yourself:

▸ What were the results?—reduced errors and faster processing

▸ Can the errors be quantified?—errors decreased from one in twenty orders to two in a hundred orders, and the time reduced from eight to two minutes per order

Here is an example of a *better* accomplishment statement:

> Reduced order entry errors from 5 to 2 percent and sped the process 400 percent by initiating, creating, and managing the implementation of a new order-entry system.

You can make it the *best* accomplishment statement by detailing the level of difficulty it took to produce the results. In this case, the new order-entry system had to meet certain criteria, such as:

▸ Integrate into the enterprise software.

▸ Process in real-time.

▸ Offer user-friendly features.

▸ Offer paperless results.

‣ Complete installation within six months on a limited budget.

Additionally, this was the first time the company used a computerized, real-time program, and the project was for a high-volume department.

Here is an example of the *best* accomplishment statement for this example:

> Reduced order-entry errors from 5 to 2 percent and sped the process 400 percent by initiating, creating, and managing the implementation of the company's first fully automated, real-time, user-friendly, paperless order-entry system in a high-volume department. Completed the project within six months with limited budget.

It will take more than a single try to develop this kind of high-quality accomplishment statement, but stay with it. In the beginning the methodology is just as important as the outcome.

Background

The final section of your résumé may contain various subsections based on your personal background. The Education subsection is required, but other subsections are included only if applicable. See Figure 2.8.

Figure 2.9 on pages 50–51 is an example of a real person's value-infused résumé. By now you should recognize all of the statements, know where they came from, and realize why they have been used. You can do the same—and develop a résumé that will get you more interviews and job offers.

How to Prepare Senior-Level Résumés

The example used thus far has been for a middle-management position in the financial services industry. The process is the same for more senior-level positions in other industries. As a demonstration, let's walk through selected steps for developing a value-infused résumé for the vice president of supply chain in a company in the food services industry.

FIGURE 2.8 *Personal background guidelines.*

Subsection	Description	Guidelines
Education	Name, city, and state of college or university and date of graduation	• List highest degree first. • Do not include GPA. • List supporting degrees only if they relate to the job or support your candidacy. • Do not list high school graduation unless you did not graduate from college. • Optionally, combine Education with Professional Development (see below). • For recent college graduates, list Relevant Coursework from most relevant to least relevant. List all the courses in which you either utilized or learned skills your prospective employer requires in the job description and/or its website. List professional development training experience related to the industry or position.
Professional Development	Detailed professional training experience related to the industry or position	• List significant external training from well-known vendors and companies, each as a separate item. • Prioritize the list according to the skills requested by the prospective employer. • Detail the skills (e.g., "Proficient in SPSS" is much better than "Proficient in data analysis"). • Use a single sentence to cover internal training from an employer. • Optionally combine this subsection with Education, especially if space is limited.
Certifications	Certifications and licenses, including dates	• List only if applicable to the industry or job position.
Community	Active or previous memberships if relevant	• List only if applicable to the industry or job position.
Affiliations	Professional associations and groups	• Be careful about including any affiliations regarding religion, politics, or other conflicting or controversial topics.
Addendum	Optionally include technical expertise, publications, patents, presentations, awards, or synopsis of previous work experience that dates back too far.	• Include any awards that differentiate yourself from other applicants and show you can excel in areas other than academia.

FIGURE 2.9 Sample résumé.

MICHELLE STREET, CPA

9501 Any Street, Chicago, IL 60600

312-555-0000 / michelle@buzztech.com

SUMMARY

Senior management financial professional with a proven record of developing future-oriented strategies that maximize shareholder value. Background includes financial management, strategic planning, marketing, and business development. A creative thinker who can bring an innovative approach to difficult business issues. An energetic and enthusiastic leader with a reputation for developing strong partner relationships and interfacing with all levels of organizations.

PROFESSIONAL EXPERIENCE

BIG SERVICE FIRM, Chicagoland, IL   **2002–2004**

The world's leading provider of market research, information, and analysis serving more than 16,000 clients in more than 80 countries.

Director, Finance, US Commercial Operations

Directed a team of six professionals in all financial planning and analysis activities for the US sales and marketing organizations, while partnering with the leaders of the US marketing and sales organizations to deliver record revenue and income in 2002 and 2003.

> Proposed and led the development of the revenue planning tool that increased sales force and finance team productivity 65 percent while increasing revenue forecasting accuracy, then organized and managed the consultant team that implemented the project. Received the 2002 Award for Excellence for this effort.

> Led negotiations for data acquisition, licensing agreement, joint ventures, and organizational restructuring that enabled the launch of a restructured US commercial organization with optimal initiatives and strategies.

> Converted a group of diversified financial technicians into an award-winning high-performance team.

ACME MARKETING COMPANY, Chicagoland, IL   **1999–2002**

Global promotions marketing firm with operations in 15 countries and annual billings exceeding $400 million.

Director, Global Business Analysis

> Led all worldwide business planning and analysis, including strategic planning, business expansions, financial planning and analysis, and mergers and acquisitions.

> Partnered with clients to design and implement the new client revenue forecasting model and financial planning package across the company, greatly improving the management team's ability to efficiently and effectively manage financial performance.

> Researched, analyzed, and presented all P&L and balance sheet forecasts in clear, concise form, projecting changes in revenue, operating income, debt levels, cash position, interest payments, and compensation calculations associated with acquisitions.

> Created and produced the company's first comprehensive global strategic plan by reengineering the process, standardizing the formats and reports, and leading the reviews with senior management and the executive board.

BIG DRUG COMPANY, Chicagoland, IL   1988–1999
Fortune 500 worldwide marketer, developer, and manufacturer of branded health-care products.

Manager, Competitive Analysis and Forecasting, Medical Products Marketing (1998–1999)
- Directed the commercial analysis and forecasting for the new development business units with annual sales exceeding $1 billion, while providing the competitive analysis activities for all business units in this $4 billion division.
- Analyzed corporate initiatives and negotiated the proposal that led to a $50 million alliance agreement between the company and an outside pharmaceutical company.
- Created an in-depth analysis of a major therapeutic category and coordinated the proper launch positioning and resources that supported the product being licensed to launch in the US. The 2002 revenues for this product exceeded $400 million.

Associate Manager, Micromarketing, Medical Products Marketing (1996–1997)
- Directed a staff of eight financial and marketing professionals in physician targeting and analysis for the marketing and sales organizations with an emphasis on ROI for the $100 million promotions budget.
- Refocused the Internet promotion spending, improving communication to target audiences, and saving $700,000 annually.
- Reengineered the promotions analysis process and vendor relationships, which cut the time of analysis turnaround from four weeks to one week while reducing analysis costs 70 percent.
- Integrated promotions planning tools into the market planning process, which provided high visibility of costs and maximized promotion spending ROI.

Early Management Positions (1988–1995)
- Starting in the Financial Professional Development Program, managed teams using continuous learning techniques in several diverse operating divisions.
- Developed the strategic project model that was adopted by all commercial teams in the $1.5 billion Hospital Care Division that streamlined investment decision making.
- Researched, analyzed, and created financial pricing and P&L proposals to ensure risks were identified and mitigated for all the major hospital buying group contracts.
- Developed and produced highly analytical commercial sales and profit forecasts for the $100 million electronic drug delivery product line.

EDUCATION, CREDENTIALS, AND AFFILATIONS
J. L. Kellogg Graduate School of Management, Northwestern University, Evanston, IL 1993–1995
Master of Management degree, with distinction, Beta Gamma Sigma, GIM study to Argentina
University of Illinois, Champaign, IL 1988
Bachelor of Science degree in finance, with honors

Certified Public Accountant, Illinois 1990

Member, Illinois CPA Society and the American Institute of CPAs
Member, American Marketing Association, Current Board Member of the Chicago Chapter

RÉSUMÉS FOR MORE SENIOR-LEVEL POSITIONS

Review the position description and company website and put the key words into categories. Since we have the position description here in Figure 2.10, we will skip the review of industry publications, save for the mention that mergers and acquisitions (M&A) have been dominant factors in the food service industry for more than twenty years. You will also notice that the key words from the company's website in Figure 2.11 call for growth "through internal expansion and strategic acquisition." The ability to perform under the pressures of mergers and acquisitions is an important factor for success and value creation in this industry. Applicants must demonstrate this value throughout the application process.

Look for M&A experience in the sample résumé as we walk through the steps of our second example. Again, you'll see that Figure 2.10 is the company's position description and that Figure 2.11 shows key words from the company's website.

FIGURE 2.10. Position description, vice president, supply chain.

Vice President, Supply Chain

ABC FOOD SERVICE CORP.

This position is responsible for the development of logistic strategies that support the ABC Snacks, Sauces & Spreads division. Forging a partnership with Sales to establish and meet customer objectives while creating value for all parties is critical. Successful execution should result in the logistic function becoming a strategic advantage to our customers.

Principal Duties and Responsibilities

▶ Coordinate and facilitate communications at the management level with issues performance and recommendations regarding logistics-related activities.

▶ Develop a consolidation strategy for the division crossing all categories and products.

▶ Develop strategies to improve and optimize freight spend and service. Implement improvement programs and track results.

▶ Provide leadership for the daily execution of transportation activities, including inbound and outbound shipments, audit freight bills, deployment of inventory and inventory reconciliations. Support efforts to deliver key Customer Service Metrics.

▶ Oversee the negotiations of truck/carrier and rail and outside warehousing contracts.

▶ Represent the Division on all ABC-wide transportation initiatives.

▶ Provide support to Sales, Marketing in rate productions, distribution recommendations, and issue resolution.

▶ Coordinate with Procurement to manage transportation efforts for inbound materials and supplies as needed to ensure timely delivery and effective cost-management.

▶ Provide cost and service reporting and analysis as needed and prepare annual transportation, warehousing, and administrative budgets.

▶ Develop and implement strategies for warehouse optimization.

▶ Develop Logistics Department Personnel.

▶ Maintain an up-to-date understanding of current regulations and trends affecting logistics-related activities. Identify and implement changes to operations, documents, agreements, etc., to facilitate continuous improvement and adherence to legal requirements.

Other Duties and Responsibilities

▶ Responsible for freight spend in excess of $70 million.

▶ Responsible for warehouse spend in excess of $35 million.

▶ Responsible for logistics network that supports over 1,100 ship-to customers, 3,000 ship-to destination points, and 120 carriers.

▶ Support 15 manufacturing facilities.

Job Qualifications

▶ BA or BS minimum degree: Logistics or business-related field with MBA preferred.

▶ 10-plus years' experience in the top logistics leadership role for a business or business unit similar to the size of ABC Food Service Snacks, Sauces & Spreads.

▶ 20-plus years' experience, including contract negotiation, carrier management, and planning.

▶ Working knowledge of DOT regulations.

▶ Strong management and interpersonal skills: 7 years' direct supervisory experience.

▶ General business background with strong analytic, financial, and facilitation skills.

▶ Strong leadership qualities—ability to build teams and influence at all levels of the organization.

▶ Strong project-management skills.

▶ Superior problem-solving and decision-making skills.

▶ Support of complex SKU structure and multiplan experience preferred.

▶ PC proficient in Windows environment, experience with Transport Management Systems a plus.

▶ Ability to travel (approximately 20%–30%).

Unlike the example from the financial services industry, this position description is not divided into convenient categories. Therefore, we had to create our own:

Planning & Strategy, Operations, Support, and Knowledge and Skills (K&S). There is no right or wrong set of categories, as they are created for your convenience. Feel free to come up with your own.

FIGURE 2.11 Key words from company's website posting.

KEY WORDS

SUPPLY CHAIN VICE PRESIDENT
ABC Food Services Corporation has proven to be not only a stable but a growing company with a management philosophy of creating shareholder value now and every day.

Growth
Through internal expansion and strategic acquisition

Leadership
Industry leader
Consistency and credibility

Market
Leading store brands (private label) and national brand strategies

We will skip the step in which the applicant is asked to list experience in reverse chronological order, as well as the entire list of statements infused with value. Here, we will share the results of those exercises by listing the actual statements (see Figure 2.12) chosen to include in the sample résumé. Note that only a few of the value-infused key words (from the list created in Step 1) are highlighted, and only a few of the quantitative/qualitative infused words are italicized. Examine the rest of the statements and see if you can determine their source and why they are included. (This will be a good test of your overall understanding of the process of value infusion.)

The statements shown in Figure 2.12 are now inserted into the sample résumé for the Vice President position, using the same format rules as discussed previously. The results are included in the sample résumé in Figure 2.13 on pages 56–57.

People with lots of experience often feel that limiting their résumés to two pages forces them to omit accomplishments they consider important. That's why the ranking and selection exercise is a critical component of developing your résumé. Far too many résumés are three and four pages in length—too many for

FIGURE 2.12 Value-infused statements—senior-level position.

- Developed and implemented strategies that rationalized and consolidated DCs and co-packers. *Reduced across-the-board cost by 25% in politically sensitive environments (union and nonunion).*

- Reorganized demand planning and supply function, reducing inventory levels by 12.5% and increasing case-fill to 99%.

- Negotiated lower cost for goods and services of internationally based contract manufacturers (Asia, US, and Canada) and reorganized team structure supporting plants, management as major factor boosting company's record earnings performance.

- Successfully led the multi-business unit supply chain divestiture team that eliminated all transition service requirements ahead of plan by 40% and exceeded targeted budget standards.

- Designed and led strategy to reduce cost of TL, LTL, and Ocean Freight by 10%; centralized load planning; and initiated a manufacturing and DC foreign trade zone that produced annual savings of $1.6M.

- Took over Logistics responsibility of newly formed business unit five months after start-up and reduced D&T spending 16%, to $73M for next budget cycle.

- Increased on-time delivery from 55 to 98% and reduced transportation cost/pound 18%.

- Conducted network study for initiatives that reduced cost by $9M and order cycle time to a maximum of seven days for refrigerated LTL network.

- Implemented S&OP process that included Demand, Supply, and senior management reviews. Spotlight focused on inefficiencies and subpar business segment performance.

- Led working capital strategy team that implemented variable inventory and replenishment strategies resulting in 14% reduction of RPW and MRO materials. *Project identified as a "Company Best Practice" for duplication elsewhere.*

- Integrated BETA Foods portfolio on time and under budget while improving productivity performance 181% in an emotionally charged environment.

- Led effort to improve daily operational execution of inbound/outbound shipments. Reduced cost/cwt 2.6% as case-pick activity increased and average order size decreased.

busy staffing people to read in full. Lengthy résumés create the impression that you are one of those applicants who likes to ramble on, wasting other people's valuable time.

Therefore, you are encouraged to keep your résumé to two pages. One way to leave the door open to discuss additional accomplishments is to add the words "Selected accomplishments include . . ." immediately before listing your value-infused statements. We have done that here, and it gives the applicant a good opportunity to discuss these accomplishments at other times during the job-application

FIGURE 2.13 Sample résumé.

TOM JONES
5555 C STREET, Chicago, IL 99999
Phone: 312-555-1212 (Cell)
321-444-1212 (Home)
E-mail: jones@gmail.com

Innovative and collaborative supply chain executive with a proven track record of design and implementation of logistics and creating value. Extensive experience leading internal and external cost initiatives with suppliers to help improve efficiencies, service levels, and EBITDA. Known for effective team building and the ability to communicate at all levels of management.

ABC SERVICE COMPANY, Chicago, IL   2007–Present
A $26.9 billion world leader in the production of manufactured metals with 63,000 employees in 31 countries servicing a wide variety of industries.

Vice President, Supply Chain, Consumer Products Division
Responsible for development and implementation of strategies that make logistics a strategic advantage for all stakeholders (including customers) through the aggressive management of freight spend, warehouse optimization, and the daily execution of operations. Selected accomplishments include:

▸ Developed and implemented strategies that rationalized and consolidated DCs and copackers. Reduced across-the-board cost by 25% in politically sensitive environments (union and nonunion).

▸ Reorganized demand planning and supply function, reducing inventory levels by 12.5% and increasing case-fill to 99%.

▸ Negotiated lower cost for goods and services of internationally based contract manufacturers (Asia, US, and Canada) and reorganized team structure supporting plants, copackers, and third-party manufacturers. Team's structure recognized by senior management as major factor boosting company's record earnings performance.

▸ Successfully led the multi-business unit supply chain divestiture team that eliminated all transition service requirements ahead of plan by 40% and exceeded targeted budget standards.

▸ Designed and led strategy to reduce cost of TL, LTL, and Ocean Freight by 10%; centralized load planning; and initiated a manufacturing and DC foreign trade zone that produced annual savings of $1.6M.

AMERICAN CANDY COMPANY   2005–2007
World's largest confectionery company with 10% global market share build on a broad geographical spread as the number one or number two in the world's top confectionery markets.

Vice President, Logistics and Consumer Operations
Responsible for Distribution, Demand and Supply Planning, Contract Manufacturing, and overall S&OP. Selected accomplishments include:

▸ Took over Logistics responsibility of newly formed business five months after start-up and reduced D&T spending 16%, to $73M for next budget cycle.

▸ Increased on-time delivery from 55 to 98% and reduced transportation cost/pound 18%.

▸ Conducted network study for initiatives that reduced cost by $9M and order cycle time to a maximum of seven days for refrigerated LTL network.

▸ Implemented S&OP process that included Demand, Supply, and senior management reviews.

▸ Spotlight focused on inefficiencies and subpar business segment performance.

CONSUMER FOOD COMPANY   2001–2005
One of the largest food and beverage companies headquartered in the US with a presence in over 150 countries, $42 billion in sales, and over 100,000 employees worldwide.

Director, West Region Supply Chain
Hired by Consumer Food to lead regional supply chain operations (53 employees) and integrate acquired logistics network of BETA Foods. Responsible for internal and external supply chain functions including Third-Party Operations across three mixing centers. Selected accomplishments include:

▸ Led working capital strategy team that implemented variable inventory and replenishment strategies resulting in 14% reduction of RPW and MRO materials. Project identified as a "Company Best Practice" for duplication elsewhere.

▸ Integrated BETA Foods portfolio on time and under budget while improving productivity performance 181% in an emotionally charged environment.

▸ Led effort to improve daily operational execution of inbound/outbound shipments. Reduced cost/cwt 2.6% as case-pick activity increased and average order size decreased.

BETA FOODS   1996–2001
One of the world's largest food-processing and -packaging companies, with over $8.3 billion in sales and 50,000 employees located in 50 countries.

Joined BETA Foods out of college in Operations. Promoted five times in six years, ending as the Regional Director, Customer Service, before being acquired by Consumer Food.

University of Scranton, Scranton, PA 1991
MBA, Productions and Operations Management

Penn State University, State College, PA 1983
BS Business Logistics

Member, Voluntary Interindustry Commerce Solutions, VICS (CPFR committee) 1998–2005
Member, Council of Supply Chain Management Professionals (CSCMP)

process. But remember, value is in the eye of the beholder, and you still must focus on what is of value to your audience during later discussions.

Two additional documents—the handbill and the cover letter—are important as you begin the search for your next job and are discussed next. These are variations on the work you have already completed and are fairly straightforward. Again, the rules for putting these documents together are the same across most industries and levels.

The Handbill

The handbill is an alternative to the standard résumé. A handbill, also known as a networking profile, is used instead of a résumé when a job seeker is meeting with a referral one-on-one or is attending a structured networking event. It is particularly useful for networking as a great leave-behind when making important connections. It allows you to meet people without being treated like a job seeker. It is designed to guide the discussion in order to gather information about companies, industries, and careers. It also functions as a tool to obtain referrals to other contacts because it helps the networking contact quickly understand the goals of the job seeker.

A handbill includes the following information:

- The same header and summary as on your résumé

- Three to five accomplishment statements under a heading of "Selected Accomplishments"

- A heading for "Target Industries or Targeted Organizations," which lists generally the industries/organizations you desire

- A heading for "Potential Jobs and Roles," which describes the general roles for which you are seeking

- A heading for "Preferred Environment and Culture," which describes the type of environment you prefer (fast-paced, small business, etc.)

- A heading for "Useful Contacts," which provides categories of significant references for recommendation

Figure 2.14 is an example of a handbill for our sample middle-management position. Use the same guidelines for a senior-management position.

FIGURE 2.14 *Sample handbill.*

MICHELLE STREET, CPA
9501 Any Street
Chicago, IL 60600
312-555-0000

SUMMARY
Senior management financial professional with a proven record of identifying and assessing business opportunities and delivering high-value solutions. Background includes financial management, strategic planning, marketing, and business development. A creative thinker who can bring an innovative approach to difficult business issues. An energetic and enthusiastic leader with a reputation for developing strong partner relationships and interfacing with all levels of organizations.

SELECTED ACCOMPLISHMENTS
▸ Proposed and led the development of the revenue planning tool that increased sales force and finance team productivity 65 percent while increasing revenue forecasting accuracy, then organized and managed the consultant team that implemented the project. Received the 2002 Award for Excellence for this effort.

▸ Converted a group of diversified financial technicians using value-maximizing strategies into a high-performance global resource by setting high expectations for the department, training them in sophisticated new skills, and coaching each one on communication and presentation techniques.

▸ Partnered with clients to design and implement the new client revenue forecasting model and financial planning package across the company, greatly improving the management team's ability to efficiently and effectively manage financial performance.

▸ Created and produced the company's first comprehensive global strategic plan by reengineering the process, standardizing the formats and reports, and leading the reviews with senior management and the executive board.

▸ Analyzed corporate initiatives and negotiated the proposal that led to a $50 million strategic alliance agreement between the company and an outside pharmaceutical company.

TARGET INDUSTRIES
Large consulting firms, major pharmaceutical firms, Fortune 500 service firms

POTENTIAL JOBS AND ROLES
Director, Strategic Planning, Chief Financial Officer, Controller, Operations Leader

PREFERRED ENVIRONMENT AND CULTURE
Moderate to high growth, team oriented, challenging

USUAL CONTACTS
Senior management at any firm, corporate bankers, partners in consulting firms, corporate attorneys, executive search consultants

The Cover Letter

You must have a cover letter to accompany your value-created résumé when you send it out. To create this cover letter, you essentially repeat the exercises you have already completed. That is, you infuse the letter with the same value as your résumé by starting with what the hiring organization is looking for and making sure you speak to that goal in your letter.

Cover letters are composed of four paragraphs but are never more than a single page in length.

PARAGRAPH 1

The first paragraph is a series of brief sentences in which you let the reader know:

▸ The position you are applying for

▸ Why you are interested in the job

For example,

> The enclosed résumé is in response to your recent advertisement for a Financial Manager in Strategic Planning. I have a strong interest in this position because of the close fit between your requirements and my skills. In addition, your company's culture has been described to me as one in which I would be particularly effective in creating the kinds of outcomes for which you are looking.

PARAGRAPH 2

Then, you provide another series of brief statements, in which you:

▸ Reference your résumé and your general experience

▸ Expand on a couple of items on your résumé that speak directly to the value the hiring organization is looking for

Remember, your résumé has been prepared in direct response to this or similar positions. You now have an opportunity to bring forward additional details about your experiences that you did not have space for in the résumé. For example,

> As you can see from my résumé, I have a strong educational background, a solid record in financial forecasting and data compilation for acquisitions, and strong leadership/team-building skills. I have always been considered a "quick study" who can generate results in comparatively short time frames.

PARAGRAPH 3

Here is an opportunity to identify any related experiences that may also qualify you for further consideration—such as public speaking, writing, research, or analytical work. For example,

> You may also be interested to know that I thoroughly enjoy and have been recognized for my ability to conduct one-on-one training with fellow team members. The overall performance rating of the teams with which I have worked always ranked the highest in the company.

PARAGRAPH 4

This paragraph is your closing statement and the action step—that is, what you want others to say, do, or think as a result of your submission. The action step is most often a request to consider you for the position and to contact you. Hence, be sure to include where and how you can be reached. For example,

> I look forward to the opportunity to discuss my candidacy with you more thoroughly. I can be reached through my e-mail address or phone number (312-555-0000). Discretion is appreciated.

Our sample cover letter is featured in Figure 2.15.

Résumés for Entry-Level Jobs

We've presented the basics for résumé preparation that apply to those with some job experience. But what about those of you who need an entry-level position? This section is for college students and/or recent college graduates and their parents. If you're in this position, learning the rudiments of value creation at an early stage in your career will prove to be valuable for the rest of your working life.

FIGURE 2.15 Sample cover letter.

Michelle Street, CPA
9501 Any Street
Chicago, IL 60600
michelle@buzztech.com

November 14, 2010

Mr. Jonathan Smith
ABC Company
Box 4680
Whereverville, IL 66666

Dear Mr. Smith:

The enclosed ["attached," if sent electronically] résumé is in response to your recent advertisement for a Financial Manager in Strategic Planning. I have a strong interest in this position because of the close fit between your requirements and my skills. In addition, your company's culture has been described to me as one in which I would be particularly effective in creating the kinds of outcomes for which you are looking.

As you can see from my résumé, I have a strong educational background, a solid record in financial forecasting and data compilation for acquisitions, and strong leadership/team-building skills. I have always been considered a "quick study" who can generate results in comparatively short time frames.

You may also be interested to know that I thoroughly enjoy and have been recognized for my ability to conduct one-on-one training with fellow team members. The overall performance rating of the teams with which I have worked always ranked the highest in the company.

I look forward to the opportunity to discuss my candidacy with you more thoroughly. I can be reached through my e-mail address or phone number (312-555-0000). Discretion is appreciated.

Sincerely yours,

Michelle Street

Michelle Street

The rules you apply to develop an entry-level résumé are pretty much the same as for mid- and senior-level jobs. Be aware, however, that competition for entry-level positions can be greater than for more advanced jobs. That is because more people are likely to meet the less stringent qualifications and apply. Nevertheless, the value-infused résumé turns less stringent qualifications into an advantage for you. Employers understand that entry-level applicants have usually done less and they adjust their expectations accordingly. They do not expect you to have solved the world's problems or to have saved a company millions of dollars so early in your career. They are mostly interested in your potential—things you will likely accomplish with additional experience and training.

Companies look to see if you have created value in other areas that translate well to the value they eventually look for you to create. Just as with more senior-level positions, you can determine what a company values by reading the position description, checking its website, and reading industry publications.

The most significant differences between entry-level résumés and others are mostly in length (shorter) and format. You follow Steps 1 through 3 and pick up the remaining instructions here. Briefly we provide examples of what your Steps 1 through 3 would look like, modified for entry-level work.

The comments governing selection of the best statements (Step 4) have been eliminated because it is unlikely that you will have many accomplishment statements. Just remember that not all your accomplishment statements will find their way into your résumé. In the event that selection is necessary, use the same guidelines as those for middle- and senior-level positions, given earlier.

RULE 1: IDENTIFY THE EMPLOYER'S KEY WORDS

Just as in Step 1 earlier, you locate the position description for the job in which you are interested and follow the instructions given earlier in the chapter. For the example shown in Figure 2.16, we have chosen a consulting company because it has a track record of hiring entry-level employees with a wide variety of college degrees, including social science majors.

FIGURE 2.16 Highlighted position description (entry level).

Consultant Trainee

JOHN T. HAMILTON CONSULTING

Are you ready for what's next in your career? At John T. Hamilton our ability to help clients solve their toughest problems and achieve their missions hinges on our people. Which is why we hire staff with great minds and a passion for making a difference, and provide them with ongoing learning opportunities, a vibrant team-based culture, a comprehensive rewards package, and the chance to make an impact for our clients, our communities, and our nation.

As a John T. Hamilton consultant you'll work within teams that deliver results to our clients in areas such as Cyber Security, Analysis/Policy, Defense/Security Policy Analysis, Economic Business Analysis, Financial Reform, Intelligence and Operations Analysis, and Organization and Strategy.

Opportunities for talented individuals with knowledge and skills in the following disciplines—and many others—are available in several locations around the country:

 ▶ Business Administration

 ▶ Economics

 ▶ International Relations

 ▶ Political Science

 ▶ And all other related majors

Basic Qualifications:

 ▶ Demonstrated leadership skills

 ▶ Excellent academic achievement

 ▶ Experience acquired through internships or study abroad programs

 ▶ Possession of excellent oral and written communication skills

We are proud of our diverse environment, EOE/M/F/D/V

Students with minimal career direction could qualify for the entry-level job described in Figure 2.16. As a result, it will likely attract a large number of applicants. The good news is you probably have the credentials to be a good candidate. On the flip side, it will be more difficult for you to stand out. The most competition for the job will come from students who, over the course of their time in college, demonstrated excellent academic, analytical, and leadership skills. Do not allow the lack of career direction to deter you from high performance in areas employers will likely think are important once you graduate. That is one sure way to keep the doors of opportunity open. The key words that pertain to this job opening are listed in Figure 2.17. Examining these key words carefully and using them in your résumé automatically gives you a leg up in the application process.

This step allows you to focus on things that have value to employers—and that is not something your competitors are used to doing. Likewise, it helps you convert those words into a powerful application. With no career direction at all, you still can concentrate on creating value in areas that many employers say they have interest. It is a mistake to wait on career-driven inspiration to achieve excellence.

FIGURE 2.17 *Key words from company's website.*

John T. Hamilton

STATEMENT OF ORGANIZATIONAL PURPOSE AND VALUES
John T. Hamilton Consulting is a leading strategy and technology consulting firm that works with clients to deliver results that endure. Public and private organizations rely on us for our expertise, objectivity, and dedication to finding solutions and seizing opportunities.

Organization Purpose
We provide exceptional service to our clients.

Core Values
Professionalism, fairness, integrity, teamwork, corporate social responsibility

Before listing your experiences and infusing them with value, however, you need to categorize those words, as shown in Figure 2.18. As you review what you have done over the past few years, think in terms of categories. What were your results, knowledge, and skills used and what are the values expressed? In what way, for example, did you solve tough problems, have leadership experiences, or work as a team?

One of our favorite stories from our career-management workshops deals with a recent college graduate who had omitted her experiences as a waitress for the summer at a resort in upstate New York. As she began to think about the links between the key words and her experiences, she saw her summer job as an example of a client-facing situation, not just another job as a waitress. Her accomplishment statement turned out to be that she was the highest-grossing summer waitress in the history of the resort—a nice accomplishment that demonstrated the kind of results orientation and client-service skills that a wide variety of employers look for.

FIGURE 2.18 *Key words by category, entry level.*

Results	Knowledge, Skills, and Experience	Core Values
Solve Tough Problems	Use Educational and Computer Skills	Client Focus
Make a Difference	Leadership	Diversity
Have Impact	Oral and Written Communication	Integrity and Fairness
	College Degree	Teamwork

She got the job, worked for a couple of years, and then enrolled in a clinical psychology master's program at the University of Chicago.

We remind students that, at this stage of the game, it is not so much what job or degree you have as it is what you do with it. It is better to reorganize the inventory system of the local hot dog cart vendor than it is to serve coffee all summer in a prestigious law firm. Create value in whatever job you have.

RULE 2: USE THE ENTRY-LEVEL FORMAT AND INFUSE EXPERIENCES WITH VALUE

Here is where the entry-level résumé begins to diverge from ones for those with job experience. For convenience and ease of construction, list your experiences using a format appropriate for entry-level jobs, using a reverse chronology.

There can be as many as five sections to an entry-level one-page résumé:

1. Header

2. Education

3. Work Experience

4. Activities

5. Awards

As you will see, value infusion begins as you format your résumé.

Joe College
Home: 150 C Street, Churchill Downs, PA 11111
Campus: UNC 4912 Box 8793, Chapel Hill, NC 22222
(123) 456-7890 Cell (789) 045-6123 Home
jcollege1@unc.edu

For entry-level positions, there is no expectation that your work experience will be without gaps. Most college students will have worked summers, breaks between semesters, or intermittently during the school years, including high school. This is also a time when extracurricular activities are especially important, so be sure to list social clubs, volunteer work, and the like.

Very often, college seniors scramble to list their experiences in résumé form a few months before graduation. Most are not adept at connecting past experience with what employers are looking for; they simply haven't had enough practice, and good instruction is hard to find. So, there are some simple but important things you can do (or advise your children to do) beginning in the freshman year, even if you have no idea at that time what your career will eventually be. Indeed, from a career perspective, this is just as important (perhaps more so) as your choice of major. It is unwise to put off career preparation simply because you are uncertain about your career direction. Yet that is the number-one mistake college students and their parents make about career management. This no doubt contributes to the large percentage of students who move back home once they finish college.

The same rules apply when listing your experiences as for middle- and senior-level positions, but the emphasis is slightly different. Advanced positions require the application of skills and activities that are closely related to what is required for the job. Instead, entry-level positions involve demonstration of generic skills. Companies do not expect you to have worked for a consulting firm, but they do look for ways you have demonstrated leadership, problem-solving, or communications skills. When you infuse your generic experiences with value, you demonstrate an understanding of what the company values.

In the entry-level résumé, educational attainment is moved up on the page because the college degree is still the ticket for most white-collar jobs and it will be your most significant attainment to date. Companies want early confirmation that applicants have the minimum qualifications. Figure 2.19 is such a résumé. Notice that we have separated the GPA in the major from the cumulative GPA. This is especially important when the major GPA is higher. Similarly, the "relevant course" listed in the résumé ties into the requirements for the position. If you look carefully, you will see other aspects of the résumé that relate to key words identified in the position description and from the website.

FIGURE 2.19 Sample résumé (entry level).

Joe College
Home: 150 C Street, Churchill Downs, PA 11111
Campus: UNC 4912 Box 8793, Chapel Hill, NC 22222
(123) 456-7890 Cell (789) 045-6123 Home
jcollege1@unc.edu

EDUCATION
University of North Carolina
BA Political Science, 2010 (exp)
GPA Major 3.8 Cum. 3.7
Relevant coursework Adv. Social Science Methods & Computer Modeling (Voter turnout)
Publications: Waning Parental Influence: Political Attitudes of Students at UNC (in Departmental Papers)

Bronx City High School, Bronx, New York
May 2006
Debate Team, National Honor Society

EXPERIENCES
Resident Advisor
September 2007–Present
> Taught suicide recognition and prevention: Participated in diversity training and leadership awareness. Member of campuswide leadership caucus that surfaced issues and crafted solutions for attention and implementation by the campus administration.

Volunteer & Leadership
Obama for President Campaign Volunteer, Summers 2006 & 2007
Campaign worker, Iowa and Pennsylvania
> Used voter preference research methodology to determine focus of campaign get-out-the-vote strategy—confirmed by headquarters and implemented by fieldworkers.

Volunteer soccer coach and mentor, 2007–2008
> Inner-city program for 4th and 5th graders in Chapel Hill, NC. Team recognized as most effective in the city for attitude changes about education and teamwork.

ADDITIONAL INFORMATION
Winner, "Most Promising Student Award" 2008, Department of Political Science; Computer proficiency—Apple, Windows, all MS office applications

Study Abroad Program, spring 2008, University Automoma de Barcelona

Fluent in Spanish, Conversational Mandarin

Let's Go Find a Different Job

Congratulations. You understand the steps to take in creating a great value-infused résumé for any level of job appropriate to your interest and background. In the process, you learned a great deal about value creation—a way of thinking that applies across the entire spectrum of career management and job search. However, some of you may be hesitant because along with looking for that next job you are also interested in changing careers. You wonder whether what you have accomplished has relevancy to a new type of position or a position in a new field or industry.

If you are considering a career change, you will probably need to develop a functional, rather than chronological, résumé. Appendix D is a sample of such a résumé format. The same principles apply, however. That is, you need to infuse your résumé with value. That can be a particular problem for a career changer because you must convince those responsible for hiring that you are more worthy than competitors whose credentials fit the position more closely.

The idea that you bring more to the table than other applicants may require a leap of faith few companies are willing to make. Your chances are improved, however, by demonstrating that the value you created in other positions effectively translates to the value someone wants you to create now. This has been done with great effectiveness by many others, but it requires planning and a careful presentation of your credentials. You cannot expect that companies will help you change careers simply because you want to. You need to convince them you are the right person for the job.

MAKING A RADICAL CHANGE

What if what you have done does not translate well to what you now want to do? If you cannot make the case to be hired over all others based on previous work, don't expect the company to make it for you. The gap between the value you have created in the past and what you want to create now has to be filled in other ways—perhaps through pro-bono work and/or additional education. For example, if a position requires project-management experience, look to working in a volunteer capacity through your social/religious affiliations, other social volunteer groups, or temp work. Once you have that experience, the link can be more obvious.

There are a number of situations in which outsiders—those without the requisite experience—are brought in to shake things up. It happened fairly often in the financial services and medical professions in the 1990s and is still happening today. For example, at one time bank employees never thought of what they did as sales. Loans were thought to be granted on the basis of personal character and asset strength; bankers were more order takers than business developers. When deregulation arrived, banks wanted people who knew how to sell their financial products.

Should I Consider a Résumé-Writing Service?

We put this question at the end because you now know about value creation and its application to writing a résumé. Finding help writing a résumé is easy—just do an Internet search on "résumé-writing services" and you'll get a long list of people and organizations. You will discover at least three professional associations, all of whom have quality assurance certifications: the Professional Association of Résumé Writers and Career Counselors (PARWCC), the National Résumé Writers Association (NRWA), and Career Directors International (CDI). Hundreds of other individuals in the business have no affiliation.

Here is the bottom line: Too many job seekers cannot distinguish between a résumé that looks good and one that has strong customized content. The exercises included here provide you with the skills to produce both.

Furthermore, the basics of preparing a good résumé are just the first step in remaining relevant in a volatile job market. The base you build here will help you network, interview, negotiate, and make career choices with purpose and direction. You read earlier that value creation is more than a résumé-writing exercise. Mastering the basics puts you in control of your own career-management process.

When you use a résumé-writing service, the real guarantee is that you will get a "good-looking" document. But you will not have learned how to make the necessary adjustments to apply for other jobs in your areas of expertise. You need to know the difference between a good-looking document (i.e., one that looks nice on paper) and one that is finely tuned to address the value employers need you to create. Further, the skills you develop when you do it yourself are tremendously useful throughout the balance of the job-search and career-management process. The service, if any, you might consider is one that helps you format and wordsmith your résumé rather than one that writes it for you.

▶ ▶ ▶

The next step in any job search is to begin the application process. That process also has been mightily affected by the new rules. The next chapter will help you understand today's job market by drawing attention to some persistent myths; identifying the tools you need to move forward; and giving you a hands-on introduction to social networking—one of the most powerful job-search methods of our time.

• • • • • • • • • • *Things to Remember* • • • • • • • • • •

▶ *Value is in the eyes of the beholder—the person making the hiring decision. Your résumé is not about you.*

▶ *You can discover what companies value by reading the position description for the job of interest, checking out the company website, and reviewing industry publications.*

▶ *You need to identify an employer's key words and organize them into categories for easy reference.*

▶ *You list your experiences in reverse chronological order and infuse them with value. Quantify, qualify, and insert employers' key words where appropriate. Then select the best statements.*

▶ *You format and refine your résumé. The two major differences between entry-level résumés and others are length (one vs. two pages) and format.*

▶ *Content is more important than format. It is okay to use templates. Just make sure the content identifies the value you created and how that translates to the value they are looking for you to create.*

RULE #3

Use Social Media and Other Sites for Job Leads

THE OLD ADVICE and the new wisdom for finding white-collar work conflict with one another most dramatically when it comes to networking, or using social and business contacts to learn about job opportunities and to get your credentials in front of the employment decision makers. Indeed, understanding the networking part of a job search is as important as writing the résumé. Yet, more than any other job-search activity, networking has undergone a seismic shift, evolving from simple face-to-face contacts into a collection of techniques mostly based in the Internet. Have you kept up?

Success in a job search today is largely a matter of casting a very wide net. In fact, by using a range of Internet services, you can extend your reach to potential employers farther than at any other time in history.

The Seismic Shift in Networking Methods

For years, face-to-face networking was regarded as the most important tool in a job search because it helped uncover the hidden job market, where supposedly 60 to 80 percent of all white-collar jobs reside. Yet it is our point that a "hidden job market" doesn't exist—perhaps it never did and it never will. Why would companies keep their job openings a secret?

The myth of a hidden job market developed as an outgrowth of surveys that asked previously unemployed white-collar workers how they found their jobs. Specifically, they were asked, "Where did you hear about your last position: (a) newspaper ads; (b) radio/TV; (c) networking contact; (d) professional publication; (d) other?" The surveys consistently reported that anywhere between 60 and 80 percent of respondents indicated "networking contact." One problem with the data, however, is that it was never verified. That is, few if any attempts were made to determine its accuracy. Researchers seldom interviewed respondents face-to-face to confirm either that what they checked off on the list of options was true or that there was more to their employment stories. Because there was little incentive to do the additional research, the outplacement industry grabbed some convenient answers and ran with them. And the conclusions appeared as logical extensions of the initial data—that is, you should develop, expand, and keep your networking contacts close. And many of us worked hard doing that very thing, never realizing that the interactive nature of the hiring process was never fully explored.

The truth behind this one-size-fits-all view is that most job seekers use a wide variety of tactics to find a new job. They don't just go to the right party, and a new job posting pops up out of nowhere. In fact, job applicants find out about possible employment through a variety of techniques, including:

▶ Reading an article about the company

▶ Seeing the opening on a job board and then going through a networking contact

▶ Asking a neighbor or friend working at the company

▶ Asking neighbors or friends if they know someone working at the company

▶ Going to the company website and applying

The fact is that we still don't understand enough about the entire pattern of interactions between applicants and the companies that hire them. More important, as technology has transformed how we network now, any findings that are reported may cause you to dramatically refocus your job search, perhaps incorrectly.

The Drawbacks of Believing Half-Truths

The "experts" concluded that the most successful job-search techniques are extensions of the career-management process itself. That is, as white-collar terminations have become the norm, job-search skills have become a major part of how careers are managed. People are advised to develop their personal networks and keep them current—continually expanding their contacts and meeting with them on an ongoing basis whenever possible. According to this argument, a call to a networking contact appears less self-serving if you have stayed in touch. Your best way to find out about open positions is through your networking contacts—the ones who come from all those face-to-face networking sessions you should attend. The belief is that most jobs are never advertised (the hidden job market) and that online applications are, at best, "iffy." We are told to leave the comfort of our computers behind and start the face-to-face networking necessary to access the hidden job market.

A little knowledge can have dangerous consequences, however, especially when you need a job. Enough of this advice is true—many people do find jobs through friends—that we are not encouraged to expand our job-search strategies beyond our immediate networking circle. Yet the truth is that the more jobs you can find and apply for, the better.

Also, relying exclusively on existing contacts and on face-to-face networking has another big drawback: most of us hate that kind of socializing, especially when we have to do it face-to-face. On balance, most of us are not very good at face-to-face networking and we quit doing it the minute we find other employment.

Julie's experiences were typical. On her way to another midweek networking session in anticipation of a rumored company layoff, she commented, "Too bad networking is so important. Who wants to spend endless hours at cocktail parties talking with people you don't know and may never see again? I would rather be home with my kids." She was relieved to hear her view confirmed by a majority of business professionals.

But rather than take our word for it, we told her to search the Web for "people who hate networking" and she would find numerous comments like these:

> ▸ "I have always found meeting strangers uncomfortable."

> ▸ "It's hard to put on a cheerful face when you are worried about losing your job."

> ▸ "I never quite know what to say. I am not good at small talk."

> ▸ "I've never networked with anyone who actually had a job to offer."

> ▸ "I can never remember whom I have spoken with and whom I haven't. That's embarrassing."

Networking to find a job can be a nerve-racking experience. Yet you do it anyway. Why? Because you have been told that's where the jobs are and the stakes are too high to forgo it. But there is a better way.

Weak Ties vs. Strong Ties

The advice to have a strong personal network that you continually expand seems logical, but as it turns out that is not such good advice, after all. People who hate to network can be comforted by research done as far back as the 1970s by sociologist Mark Granovetter, who observed that weak ties between networking contacts work just as well as strong ones. It was as if Granovetter anticipated the way many of us network today, using the weak ties of Internet social-networking sites. Internet-based social-networking sites are characterized largely by "weak ties," or contacts that are casual, in contrast to the strong ties we develop with friends and associates with whom we interact in person. When we are looking for work, Granovetter argued, weak ties are actually superior to strong ones because they allow us to connect across a broader range of relationships.[1]

On average, the number of people with whom we can connect face-to-face and with whom we can maintain strong ties maxes out at around 250—and that's with a lot of work and emotional energy. By contrast, the number of people with whom we can establish weak ties is essentially limitless. This is not to argue that strong connections are not useful—they are. Yet all your connections don't necessarily have to be strong when you're looking for a job; most people get what the looser connection is all about. They are not bothered by requests for job leads; indeed, unemployment is common enough today that long explanations about what happened are no longer necessary. It is enough to say that you were with a company that "downsized," "merged," or "restructured." The point is that you can get important assistance from these people even when they are unaware of job openings and even if they do not know you personally. They can pass on your information to others.

How Companies Hire Today

It is helpful to understand how companies actually fill vacancies today. Each year CareerXroads, a highly respected staffing-strategy consulting firm, conducts a survey to determine where companies with 5,000+ employees find their new hires. Here is what it found:[2]

- *Internal transfers and promotions* made up 38.8 percent of all full-time positions companies filled, a number that ballooned to 51 percent at the height of the Great Recession—because companies reduced their outside hiring activity in favor of internal promotions.

- *Referrals* (employee, alumni, vendors, etc.) constituted 27.3 percent of positions filled, providing the most significant source of outside hires. Together, the top two categories made up 76.1 percent of all positions filled.

- *Company career sites* supplied 22.3 percent of all outside hires—but how they fit into the overall pattern of employment remains unclear. Experts in the field increasingly feel that company websites are becoming less relevant as a source of hires and more of a destination point—a place to which interested parties are directed when they want additional information about a company.

- *Job board hires* represented 13.2 percent of external hires (i.e., 13.2 percent of the 27.3 percent of external hires). In the latest findings, Monster.com was beginning to lose ground to Career Builder, and both appear to have lost ground to social networks and other online search engines that are expanding their reach.

▶ *Diversity hires* appear to come from a variety of sources, among which affinity groups (usually internal company-sponsored groups in support of various diversity efforts—females, minorities, etc.) seem to be the most important.

From this and other sources, you can see how companies (in this instance, large companies) tend to find new employees. Though care should be taken when expanding these findings to all companies, both big and small, the fact is that, in a global world, companies all face the same pressures to hire the best talent available. So, the first observation to be made from the data is the rough correlation between the expense associated with attracting new hires and the methods used. The most widely used methods are also the most cost-effective.

This draws attention to two interrelated factors: getting the right talent in the most cost-effective manner possible. The search for talent has become red-hot in response to global competitiveness. By some estimates, a third of all business failures can be traced to poor hiring decisions. The cost to replace poor performers is estimated to be 1.5 to 3 times their salaries. Furthermore, high performers outperform poor performers by 25 to 100 percent in similar jobs. In more complex positions, the gap has been reported to be anywhere from 500 to 1,000 percent.[3] So, some of the most visible companies, such as IBM, GE, Google, Apple, and Walmart, cast as wide a recruiting net as they possibly can. They understand that acquiring the right talent is far too important a task for their openings to be tucked away in the "hidden job market" or to hire-on-the-cheap.

That's because the job market today is not so much hidden as it is splintered. Job opportunities are announced in a variety of ways, scattered across different means of attracting applicants. So, just as job seekers need to look in many places for openings, companies need to post their opportunities in myriad places. For instance, companies are often unsure where to look for talent or how much to pay for their search. Those "best places" to find talent have changed recently and new preferences have emerged.

Companies are not hiding their openings; they are finding new ways to seek outstanding candidates. For example, they don't use newspaper classified ads anymore.

These ads are too expensive for companies who want to attract sufficient numbers of candidates, from whom they can select the best. The movement away from print ads has been so dramatic, in fact, that the traditional newspaper "want ads" have all but disappeared. Staffing professionals know there are better ways to find better candidates than placing ads in the *New York Times* or the *Wall Street Journal.*

The new consensus on the best ways to look for talent has the Internet as its core. In 1997, 2.1 percent of new hires came through the Internet.[4] Today, the Internet serves companies via referrals, career sites, job boards, direct sourcing, and college contacts. In fact, it no longer makes sense to survey how many new hires come through the Internet because, in one way or another, practically all do. Face-to-face networking has been exposed for what it is: an appendage to what job seekers accomplish mostly on the computer. But to succeed in this Internet-based business world, job seekers need to obtain computer literacy.

No Excuses for Not Keeping Up

If you are comfortable with—indeed, have grown up with—computers, you can skim the following material. You're poised to take advantage of the job opportunities the Internet has to offer. But for you Luddites, here's a little about computer literacy.

There is an undeniable generation gap in any discussion of computers. Younger people tend to be more proficient, more computer literate, than people over fifty. But if you are looking for employment, get online. Learn the basics. In a few years, this warning will be a lot like telling people about indoor plumbing today.

If you are uncomfortable using a computer, you need to take some classes. Try your local public library because libraries often offer cost-effective services that bring people up to speed on new developments in technology. Many community colleges also have continuing education courses on computer use, frequently in a comfortable, easy-to-learn environment.

At one time, listing your basic computer skills on a résumé was a way to distinguish you from others in the job market. Today, computer skills are a commodity that everyone is expected to have. Only more esoteric computer skills are listed now on résumés. Even those who are mildly computer literate have the challenge of keeping up—the speed at which technology changes is mind-boggling. So, any "catch-up" plans must include consideration of how you will remain current.

Changes that once played out over generations are now intragenerational. As Jerry Garfunkel noted in "The Digital Divide Between Age Groups":

> As a young boy I watched my father connect the stereo components and thought what a technological wizard he was. As a young girl, my daughter watched me scan computer listings and thought what a technological wizard I was. As a young girl, my granddaughter will watch her mother create web pages and broadcast them around the world, and she too will think what a technological wizard her mother is.[5]

You are advised to get on the right side of the digital divide and eliminate it as an age-related consideration. You should focus more on the value you create than on age, regardless of how old or young you are. When you create value that others need, the impact of age is reduced to a less significant consideration.

Our initial meeting with an outplacement client typified the digital divide. After an exchange of pleasantries, Dan was asked, "So, tell me about yourself." For the next forty-five minutes, he gave us an uninterrupted stream of stories about how his former company had replaced older workers with younger ones and his concern was that he would face more of the same as he conducted his job search. This fifty-five-year-old had a skill set that was being replaced by a foreign, younger, more highly skilled workforce that also happened to be less expensive.

We have heard this story from lots of people, and yet many do not take responsibility for keeping up with technology. Our advice to these clients is that they follow the lead of Satchel Page, the legendary Hall of Fame baseball player who spent his youth toiling in the Negro Leagues before reaching the majors well past his prime. During those years, reporters always wanted to know how old he was. But he never gave a straight answer. He would instead respond with one of his trademark witticisms, "Age is a case of mind over matter. It you don't mind, it don't matter." We cannot promise that age won't matter. But we can say with confidence that if you stay current with technology and learn to create value, it will matter a lot less.

Are you keeping up or falling behind? Is it time to take some computer classes? Following is a simple test to help you determine that. For every yes response, you get one point.

A Computer-Literacy Test

Do you:	YES	NO
1. Have daily access to a high-speed line?		
2. Have a high-speed line in your home?		
3. Do you read newspapers primarily online?		
4. Do you do online banking?		
5. Do you shop online?		
6. Do you make travel reservations online?		
7. Do you belong to an online social-networking group?		
8. Do you own a Web-enabled cell phone?		
9. Do you have a Facebook account?		
10. Do you download music?		

Score/Status

10–9: Considered literate and keeping up

8–7: Literate, but be careful not to fall behind

6 & below: A candidate to take some classes

Where You Should Look for Jobs

Many people report being confused about the advice they get when it comes to job applications. As an example, Caroline spent three months of unproductive time responding to job ads. Her outplacement firm provided the clerical support necessary for her to respond by personal letter or e-mail within ten business days after an opening was posted. She also filed several applications online. Later, Caroline learned that the success rate for this kind of activity was 7 percent or less. "Why," she asked, "was I told to spend so much time doing this when it had almost no chance of landing a job?"

As an alternative, Caroline was advised to get away from her computer, strengthen her face-to-face networking ties, and follow the leads developed there. The advice seemed logical, largely because of what we have heard about job searches. Yet, it also didn't work.

If companies are willing to go to the trouble and expense of listing their job openings online or elsewhere, why are job seekers told not to respond? We know that when a single ad attracts as many as fifty résumés, the process becomes a numbers game, with a guaranteed low rate of success. When only one person in fifty can get the job, only 2 percent of all applicants will win overall. When the number of applicants is even higher, as it often is, the percentages are even lower. But the conclusion that you should therefore avoid responding to these ads is a complete mistake. Job seekers need to have a good idea of where to look for open positions, regardless of where they appear or what the initial chances are of landing them.

As we discussed earlier, conducting an effective job search has to do with creating value for your potential employer. With that in mind, let's review where to look for openings and what to do when you find them. Here are some obvious and not-so-obvious places to find job opportunities:

1. *Your current or former employer.* Some companies want nothing to do with former employees and they stop formal communications except on matters of benefits and other legal obligations. It is not unusual for the outplacement firm to replace the former company as the primary point of contact. However, companies are becoming smarter. Many now understand that former employees ("boomerangs," they are called) are an excellent reservoir of talent to meet future staffing requirements, as well as positive sources of good public relations among their ever-widening Internet circle of friends. A polite request to be kept in mind for future consideration or to provide job leads is a good idea. Also, well before any hint of a layoff, be sure your personal brand is highly respected and your name is among the first your current employer will think about if an opportunity for reemployment or promotion comes along. How do you accomplish this? Learn to create value and be sure not to burn bridges as you exit. Your chances of reemployment with a previous employer are enhanced if you are capable, respected, and well liked.

2. *The position description you used to develop a value-infused résumé.* In order to develop a competitive résumé you had to come up with a job description of a current vacancy. Apply for that job, and if it is filled, get your credentials in front of the company's management anyway. It doesn't hurt for them to know who you are and how well your background fits their recruiting requirements at the time.

3. *Jobs that are listed with your friends and family.* This is the old-fashioned face-to-face networking that was the advised route years ago, and it still is a viable path. Though you will learn how to go well beyond this narrow circle of contacts, friends and family can be a good source for uncovering job leads that may not have come to your attention. But this is not because the jobs are hidden. There are still many channels through which jobs are listed, and you should let this network know you are looking for work and are interested in any information it may come across. As you become more computer savvy, your network will grow into a wider network of contacts primarily through the Internet's weak ties.

4. *Company websites.* As companies become more sophisticated about the Internet, they use their own websites to replenish their list of candidates for current and future openings. For large companies, in particular, it is a cost-effective way of reaching out to a widely dispersed pool of potential candidates. One client was surprised to see that the supply chain vice president's position he had been contacted for by a search firm was also listed on the company's website. "Why," he asked the hiring manager, "would you list the job on your website and also pay a search firm to come up with candidates?" As it turns out, the job of the search firm was to rank-order *all candidates* regardless of the source of application. Drawing quality applicants from the website was an inexpensive and positive net addition to the process.

5. *Trade magazines.* Jobs are listed in trade magazines because employers are trying to reach specialized populations with specific skill sets or people who have specialized training. Depending on how frequently the magazine is published, job leads are sometimes stale. Increasingly, trade magazines have added an online dimension to their recruiting activity to overcome the limitations of infrequent publishing schedules for hard-copy editions. Some have even eliminated the hard copy altogether and operate completely online.

6. *Jobs listed at professional conventions/meetings.* Professional conventions are a favorite among the job-search crowd because of the chance to meet others in their profession and get to know them informally or through more formal channels such as professional committees, presentations of papers, or participation on panels. These gatherings invariably have "job boards" that give applicants a chance to inquire about opportunities, both formally and informally.

7. *College placement centers and their alumni groups.* Placement centers have been slow on the uptake in providing services to their alumni. Most colleges and universities have a significant cadre of alumni who would find opportunities for midcareer counseling and job leads helpful. Companies with strong college-recruiting ties to a particular university would also be welcome participants at forums that allow them to reach out to experienced workers who know how to create the kind of value they seek. Short of more formal programs, college placement centers and their alumni groups are spots where jobs are listed and candidates connect with companies looking for talent.

8. *The state unemployment office.* Though jobs are routinely listed here, this source is often overlooked. That is a mistake, especially for those interested in changing careers and looking for opportunities to display their transferable skills.

9. *Cities with strong economies.* It is easier to find work in some cities than in others. If you are able to relocate, you should know what cities offer the best prospects for finding a job. During the Great Recession, Washington, D.C., and Jacksonville, Florida (in the top ten best cities for finding work), had significantly lower unemployment rates than did Buffalo, Orlando, Sacramento, and Chicago (among the worst cities for finding a job). Even when the employment outlook is positive in areas unrelated to your expertise, the local economic multiplier effect will broadcast through the local economy.

10. *Newspaper ads.* Though waning in influence, local newspaper ads still represent a good source for job listings. Local companies likely prefer local candidates for a variety of reasons, including that the references are easier to check; relocation from another city or state may be unreliable; face-to-face communication is easier; and the candidates can be less expensive to recruit.

11. *Private employment agencies, including retained search and contingency firms.* The distinctions between search and contingency firms are fading fast. Retained search firms were once used for higher-level positions and were paid for by the company whether someone was placed or not. Contingency firms were used for lower-level positions, and a fee was paid "contingent" on the agency's candidate getting the job. Both types of firms are still excellent sources of job listings. Connect with someone who can act as a reference to search consultants inside the search firms. Search consultants can receive as many as 200 unsolicited résumés a day, and of necessity they pay attention to only those that are a fit with current assignments. A referral from a trusted friend or someone with whom you are casually connected through others will increase your chances of a courtesy response and a promise to "keep your résumé on file should something develop." If you are able, establish an ongoing relationship with a search consultant by acting as a reliable source of candidates for other positions. That is, create value for the consultant whenever you can. Be aware, however, that these consultants live in an "out of sight/out of mind" world and touching base from time to time is often necessary to remind them of who you are and the value you offer.

12. *Civil service.* Don't forget the federal government. For many professionals, it is an excellent source of job listings and often a secure employer. That advice should also extend to local and state governments. If you have not kept up, you may not know that 80 percent of all civil service positions are filled through a review of your background, work experience, and education rather than via a written exam. The point is, the government has a list of open positions and readily seeks outstanding candidates.

13. *Temp agencies.* Temporary-agency employment activity is a leading indicator of economic growth. As such, many employment opportunities early in an economic recovery cycle emerge as temporary positions. The old days in which these jobs were strictly clerical in nature are gone. Temps now come in all shapes, sizes, and managerial levels, up to and including CEOs. Take advantage of temporary assignments to create outstanding value for the companies in which you work. Going from "temp" to "perm" is a real possibility once they have seen your work and have a clear idea of its quality.

14. *Online job postings/job boards.* Remember the good old days when conventional wisdom held that you could not find a job on the Internet? Those who are critical of the Internet as a job-search tool simply misunderstand both its power and how to use it. In reality, the Internet is a source of job listings like no other that has ever existed. Job boards are part of the emerging staffing technologies attracting the attention of staffing professionals and the companies they represent. Among current job boards, CareerBuilder, Monster, HotJobs, and Craigslist lead the pack in sources of hires. More narrowly targeted job sites such as DICE and The Ladders have less market share because they cater to more selective audiences.

15. *Yellow Pages.* Jobs are listed in many ways, and one of the simplest sources of information is the Yellow Pages, either online or the physical book. The Yellow Pages contains listings of businesses that are trying to attract business; successful ones need new people, and some job seekers have found success with these growing companies.

16. *Self-employment.* For many, self-employment is the ultimate job listing. Once you understand value creation in its fullest sense, self-employment becomes a realistic option for expanding that reach to a full-time position. As stated earlier, self-employment often comes with a higher-risk profile.

This is intended to be a good start rather than an exhaustive list. Do not be confused: where jobs are posted has little to do with how you should go after them. Once they are found, your success in landing the job depends on a number of factors that can be ranked from best to worst. Let's see where you stand.

The Job-Search Pyramid

Have you ever noticed how some people always seem to be in demand? They never have to look for a job. They are the first ones companies and search consultants think of when the vacancies occur. And if they are not interested, their opinion is sought as to who might be a good candidate. It isn't that they never get fired. They do. But finding the next assignment is seldom a major source of anxiety for them. These people are not in the best position for every job they go after, but they are often enough that others wonder, "What do they know that I don't?"

Here is the secret. Throughout their careers, and in every job circumstance, these people push themselves as high as they can up to higher levels of a pyramid of job seekers. The good news is that with value creation, you can do the same. Furthermore, you don't need to be successful all the time or in every job you ever have. Like other skills, you need only to get better than you currently are and improve your "hit rate" on interviews for the jobs you decide to apply for.

The Job-Search (JS) Pyramid (see Figure 3.1) is a visual representation of the job-search process. You can use it to determine what level you are at and what options are available to move you up the pyramid.

Let's consider the five levels of the pyramid.

INSIDE PROMOTIONS AND LATERAL MOVES

At the very top of the pyramid, these opportunities exist where you work and where the value you create has already been recognized. This is the most desirable of the job-search situations and the position most of us prefer. An organization has

FIGURE 3.1. Job-Search Pyramid.

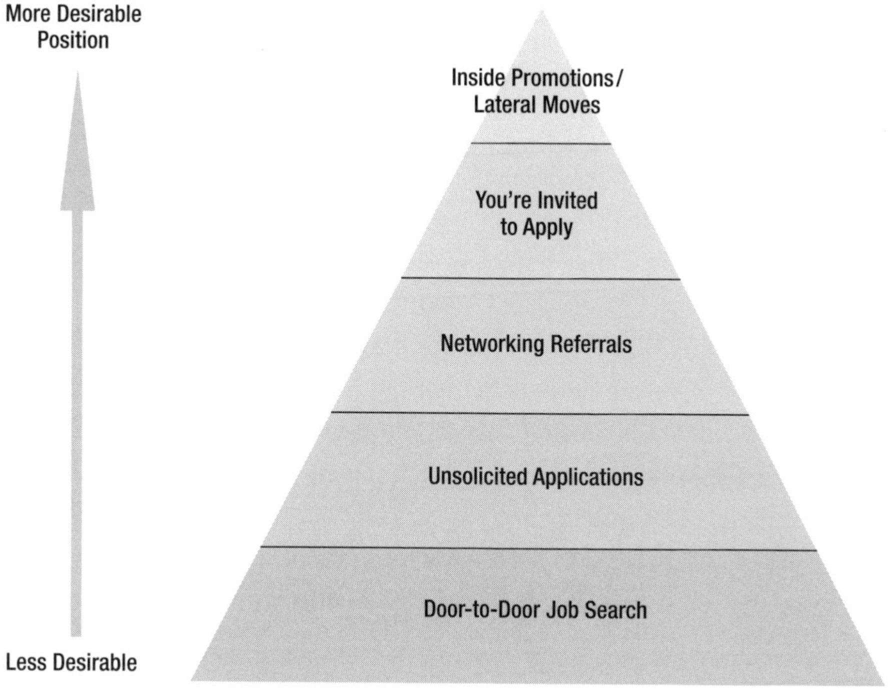

More Desirable Position

Inside Promotions/ Lateral Moves

You're Invited to Apply

Networking Referrals

Unsolicited Applications

Door-to-Door Job Search

Less Desirable

reflected on the skills it needs and has identified those who most closely fit the bill—and chose you. Lateral moves are included here because they are opportunities to gain additional experience, as well as demonstrate your ongoing ability to create value in other situations—a significant accomplishment in these times of flat organizational structures and the reduced number of promotions that accompany them. Even if you do not want to stay with the organization, or are ambivalent about the new position being offered, you can always turn it down. But having a job offer or a chance to move laterally is a good result. There may be times when you would prefer not to take a lateral move. It is still a positive in that you are able to advertise your brand in the job market as having been offered other positions you chose to turn down.

Do lateral moves and promotions really count as job searches? Yes, they do. When you treat your current employment situation as a job search, it is a constant reminder that all jobs—past and present—are opportunities to enhance your personal brand. How you are treated by your employers is also important content for your résumé; you can list promotions and other career moves as indicators of your ongoing ability to create value.

The one surefire way to position yourself for a promotion is to be a star performer. Do this throughout your educational experience and in each job assignment you take on. You will also find that "stars" very often don't need résumés. Well-run companies know who they are, and job opportunities seem to find them without effort. Think of it this way: If you are Lebron James and want to play for some other professional basketball team, no one is going to ask you for your résumé. What you have already accomplished is well known and need not be summarized in a résumé. Organizations know who the stars are and treat them as such.

As the competition for talent continues, successful companies will likewise be those that know who the stars in their industry are and what it takes to attract and retain them. Many Silicon Valley companies have understood this competitive process for years and have pioneered innovative hiring practices in response. As an example, one company not only has an on-site day-care center with desktop TV access for parents to keep a watchful eye on children, but also provides grandparents (on request) with a password to observe the kids from their computers at home.

But until you reach undisputed star status, and enough companies are tracking your career, a well-written résumé is still the best way to summarize your accomplishments and the value you create.

YOU'RE INVITED TO APPLY

Unsolicited invitations from another company or search firm are the next most desirable situations. They have heard of your work and feel as if your candidacy makes sense. This process is less certain than internal promotions or lateral moves because candidates are sometimes used to "round out" candidate slates as "stalking horses" but may not be serious contenders. Still, you are on the inside of the search—a desirable position under any circumstance and an opportunity to strut your value-creation skills. You have a chance to focus on the value that the hiring organization is looking to have created and to relate that specifically to the value you have created during your career. You do not have to network your way into the situation—you are already on the inside.

NETWORKING REFERRALS

For those unfamiliar with social networking, this rung will have the look and feel of traditional face-to-face contacts. This is not necessarily so! More than ever before, we are able to network to contacts through a series of weak ties for jobs and information, including who the real decision makers are; the ins and outs of the culture of a company; why a certain position is vacant; what a company hopes to accomplish in filling a vacancy; and a lot more. These are all aspects of the job that help you connect to the right people with a résumé tailored to meet their needs. From time to time you will be able to connect directly with a networking referral, but at other times you will not. Your chances are directly tied to the kind of personal brand you have established, the value you create, and how fully you have developed your network. Those who have done these things more completely than others will be able to locate information that enhances their application and subsequent chances of successfully landing that next position.

UNSOLICITED APPLICATIONS

This is the level where most of us stand with the typical vacancy. At this level, we have two options: try to get repositioned up the JS Pyramid or accept where we are.

To move up the pyramid at least one level requires job-centered networking with family, friends, and a wider set of contacts through social-networking websites such as LinkedIn, Facebook, or Twitter.

These three sites in particular currently are great sources for networking your way in as a candidate. Be aware that other social-networking sites and applications are developed every day. Becoming computer literate and keeping up is a conscious decision each of us has to make as we continue to leverage technology. The best way to keep up is to become a constant user. Moving up a single rung on the pyramid is all but guaranteed, and moving to the highest levels over time becomes a distinct possibility.

At this level, sometimes moving up the pyramid is inconvenient or simply too difficult. In this case, you are left with sending out résumés en masse. Should you ever really do that? Submitting a value-infused résumé still enhances your chances of recognition and of obtaining a first-round interview. By using a social-networking site such as LinkedIn, you can often connect directly with the hiring manager or with someone who knows the hiring manager and can refer you. But you still are one of a large number of relatively unknown applicants, with a long shot for making it to the next round. However, if this is the only strategy you have, and you also have a value-infused résumé, go with it. You can improve your response rate from mass mailings.

A few years ago, Laura, then a recent graduate of the University of California, Davis, with limited social-networking contacts and a strong desire to get a job without the help of family, worked with us to develop her résumé. In spite of a weak economy, she quickly got several job interviews through unsolicited responses to posted vacancies. Having more choices than she anticipated, she was able to choose a job that was a good fit and remains employed there today—several promotions later.

DOOR-TO-DOOR JOB SEARCH

At this level you are looking for unknown or future vacancies. It's a tough way to go and not everyone can do it effectively. You must draw up a list of businesses (from the Yellow Pages, for example), identify companies that can use your skill set, and check with each one about vacancies it may have. This procedure can be done door to door, on the phone, or over the Internet. Don't forget, 2.5 percent of all hires in the CareerXroads survey came from unsolicited walk-ins. Though you get a lot of nos, you need only a single yes to make the effort worthwhile.

Social-Networking Success

Ample evidence shows that the popularity of social networking is growing at breakneck speed. Although the social-networking sites were once considered a quirky niche for nerds and college students, by 2009 54 percent of the Fortune 100 companies had Twitter accounts, 32 percent had corporate blogs, and 29 percent had a Facebook fan page.[6] The numbers are expected to explode upward. Over half of the direct-sourcing hires counted in the CareerXroads survey came from LinkedIn.[7]

Furthermore, the Internet itself is changing. The idea of sitting in front of one's computer is passé—not because you can't find a job there but because we routinely have Internet access through our personal digital assistants (PDAs), and an increasing number of social networks send information directly to our mobile phones.

How fast is social networking growing? In the beginning months of 2009, Facebook reached the milestone of 175 million users—not a bad rate of growth for a social-networking site started in 2004 that was initially limited to college students with a university/college e-mail address. In some weeks, Facebook grew by more than 600,000 users per day, and by December 2009, Facebook usage had grown to 350 million, with most users no longer just college kids; 45 percent of its membership was twenty-six years old and higher. The fastest-growing segment of Facebook in the United States was women over fifty-five. And Facebook had expanded to over fifty-two countries, as well. Furthermore, the growth numbers of users of other social-networking sites, such as LinkedIn, MySpace, and Flickr, are impressive as well.

However, the Internet is replete with exaggerated claims about what social networking can do for your job search. For example, perhaps you heard the story about a software engineer who lost his job on Friday afternoon and eleven days later had another one. How did he do this? He sent word of his job situation to his network, their friends, and friends of theirs. These results, however, are not representative of what you will experience using similar methods.

For example, consider the situation presented by myhusbandneedsajob.com. In May 2008, Michael Stearns graduated with an MBA from Georgetown University and relocated to San Francisco in hopes of finding a job in corporate marketing.

Several months later, his wife gave his job search substantial visibility when she launched a new website, myhusbandneedsajob.com, on which she posted Michael's résumé, pictures of themselves, and several other comments extolling his virtues. The website went viral—that is, it became a destination point for millions of visitors. Yet over a year later, no job was in sight.

Newcomers to social networking are advised that the name of the game continues to be value creation. Social networking can play an enormously important role in helping you get the word out, but in the long run it cannot act as a substitute for the value you create. The *quality* of your brand still counts. Social networking simply brings that quality to the attention of a wide circle of contacts.

What do you need to get started? Social networking is neither a mature set of practices nor an established invention with an agreed-upon meaning for everyone. People constantly bend it to meet their needs and make it what they want. The best way to learn the ropes is to pay close attention to how others do it. Some of the early books that sought to teach people how to navigate the more popular sites went quickly out of date because the rules for usage kept changing. We do not intend to make that mistake. Therefore, here are the basics.

What Is Social Networking?

For our purposes, social networking "is the spontaneous movement of people using online tools to connect, take charge of their own experience, and get what they need—information, support, ideas, products, and bargaining power from each other."[8] Conveniently, people can go to a site to do their social networking or they can create their own. Technology allows people to connect in ways and around issues they could not connect before. It also allows them to take control of their own brand and what others read and hear about them—what they have accomplished and the value they have created. So, don't keep your light hidden under a basket. Social networking will allow you to toot your horn in earshot of as many people around the globe as are interested in what you have done or have to say.

Social-networking activity can be broken down into four classifications and many social-networking sites use features from more than one category:

1. *Community social-networking sites.* These make up the largest category, and they are used by members to help them grow their number of connections. People find existing contacts (e.g., high school classmates) and make new ones (friends of your high school classmates with autistic children). People can begin to share information on effective parenting techniques, organizations that provide emotional support and counseling, new developments in treatments, and so on. The benefit of such a network is obvious and individuals have opportunities to demonstrate their expertise (value) in numerous ways.

2. *Media sites.* The main activity on these sites is to upload photos and videos for others to see. For those who feel as if they have something of value to say or view, media sites can be particularly useful. From time to time, uploaded music videos in particular take off and become viral hits. Such was the case for a couple of Yale students whose rendition of Lady GaGa's "Poker Face" became their second viral hit, with more than 1.5 million viewers. Perhaps the most famous of all viral hits happened with Susan Boyle's appearance on the popular TV show *England's Got Talent.* It attracted a whopping 50 million viewers, and counting—not possible without social networking. Music-sharing sites (music social networks) are a subset of media sites and shortly may become their own category because of the way they are used and how quickly they are evolving.

3. *Social bookmarking sites.* Bookmarking happens when you save a link to a website in your Web browser. Social bookmarking is saving the same link where others can see what you are bookmarking. You can then "tag" the sites with as many words as you choose. Because of the tremendous number of websites, there is value in gaining a reputation for locating and tagging sites others find of value.

4. *Blogging social networks.* These are sites that bring bloggers together. They allow you to find other bloggers ("blog" is short for Web log) in which you have an interest and communicate and exchange blogs as desired. Many feel that Facebook sites will become tomorrow's newspapers—places to obtain information on a variety of topics and a wide range of opinions.

Getting Started

To get started, focus on three major sites: LinkedIn, Facebook, and Twitter—in that order. LinkedIn comes with our highest recommendation because it is specifically designed for business professionals. It links people for purposes of career management and business development, and is a direct challenge to the notion someone cannot find a job on the Internet.

Facebook was developed with a broader purpose in mind—to put people in touch, share photos, and allow you to meet new people easily. Twitter is a social media site that allows users to send short updates of what they're doing and converse about their interests in 140 characters or less. Many use it online through the Twitter website but it can also be used through a smartphone app, through text messages, or through another third-party application for desktops and laptops.

Though it is common practice to use all three of these social-networking sites in conjunction with one another, their differences are important. Most of what attracts people to Facebook and Twitter has nothing to do with finding a job. As a result, more work is required if you want to use them for that purpose.

The best way to learn is to plunge right in and see how other people use these sites. But you should not jump in the deep end first. Start with networking sites and activities that will improve your familiarity while keeping you from making foolish errors. To be on the safe side, you may want to join a self-help group to see how members use social networking and then proceed. The power of social networking comes largely from what users, not owners, make of it. You need to proceed with caution until you gain greater clarity about what you are trying to accomplish and how a particular site can facilitate your objectives.

LINKEDIN

A social-networking site for business professionals, LinkedIn is for those who want to find jobs, sales leads, business partners, and much more. In addition, LinkedIn makes it easier for the jobs to find you. In this sense, the site helps you move higher up on the Job-Search Pyramid. So far, it is among the safest of all social-networking sites with which to experiment because its primary purpose is to facilitate business/professional connections. By 2010, LinkedIn boasted over 50 million users worldwide—by far the most extensive network devoted to business professionals.

You participate on LinkedIn by joining—you visit the site (www.linkedin.com) and fill out a profile. It's free. You are then on your way. You should take as much care in building your profile as you did in developing your résumé. In fact, your

LinkedIn profile is considered your online résumé. Companies and other business contacts will be attracted to you based on the value you create, and your profile will often be the very first impression you make on them. Make it a good one. But don't worry about it just yet. You will get better at building your profile once you join and see how others do it. You can go back and edit what you have written at any time. The important thing is to get started. Here's how:

1. *Develop contacts.* Identify your contacts by uploading your e-mail contact list and conduct searches for colleagues, classmates, and individual names. These come from your profile. LinkedIn identifies others who have joined who may be connected to you because they went to the same schools, worked for the same company, lived in the same towns, and so on.

2. *Convert contacts to connections.* Direct LinkedIn to invite selected contacts of your choice to join your network. For a connection to happen, someone must accept your invitation, just as you must accept other invitations to join someone else's network. If the person refuses (or you refuse to accept an invitation), LinkedIn won't tell. The same is true if you decide to disconnect. Unlike other social-networking sites, connection means that you know these individuals well and are willing to be one degree of separation from them. It also allows you to see whom your contacts are connected to. There is a special feature that prohibits even those you are connected to from viewing your other contacts. Senior-level search consultants and other highly placed people use this feature to prevent being inundated with requests to connect to highly visible executives.

The people you are connected to are considered to be one degree of separation from you. The connections of your contacts are then two degrees removed, and their direct connections are three degrees from you. Conveniently, LinkedIn can tell you who in your network are one, two, or three degrees of separation from organizations or individuals you may have an interest in. This allows you to network your way through to many places you would not normally have access to.

To contact second- and third-degree connections requires special LinkedIn tools—Introductions, InMail, or OpenMail. You will learn how those work once you join. For purposes of getting started, all you need to know is that LinkedIn provides five free introductions with a free LinkedIn account. You can buy more introductions by upgrading to a premium account for a modest monthly fee.

Users can look at the connections of their direct contacts to find a link to someone they want access to. If that's your case, you can then request an introduction to a second-degree contact. Your contact can either pass it along or not, and that connection can either accept it or not. Refusing the introduction can be done anonymously. Accepting an introduction is not the same as becoming a part of someone's network. That requires an invitation and a corresponding acceptance. Sound confusing? It is really quite simple, as will become obvious once you get started.

Once you join, take time to get familiar with LinkedIn's functions. Go to the page where your account is housed and browse. You will discover a number of navigational buttons that allow you to use LinkedIn more aggressively—everything from editing your profile to seeing whom your contacts are connected to, groups to join, and much more. In your spare time, you will find it helpful to browse and see how many new things there are to be discovered. One tab in particular to explore is "Jobs." Job seekers can search and apply for as many jobs as they want— it's free and you apply directly to hiring managers or those managing the search. To post a job, however, costs about $200. Jobs are organized by geographical region, and the system will tell you which jobs are connected to you and by how many degrees, giving you opportunities to do some focused networking through those weak ties that have traditionally been ignored.

James found his new job using the method suggested above. He had an excellent personal brand—an MBA from a well-known school and several years of solid work experience. He targeted several financial services institutions and identified the friends of his friends who were employed by those companies. Eventually he worked his way into a courtesy interview and was offered a position shortly thereafter.

Another important navigational button is "Groups." Here, you can join or create groups and participate in discussions around your areas of interest or expertise. You can refer participants to your blog on a given subject (if you have a blog), post comments that further highlight your interests and expertise, and/or draw attention to what others have written by copying and pasting links to other sites.

On the flip side, companies pay LinkedIn handsomely to comb their considerable database for "passive" candidates (those who might be interested but are not actively looking). Carefully written profiles that show solid track records of success and sensitivity on issues that are important to your industry or profession will likely bring your credentials to the attention of others and move you higher up the JS Pyramid.

The process by which a company combs a database of potentially millions of candidates involves searches for key words that are easily embedded in the résumés and profiles of LinkedIn subscribers. This takes you back to the initial exercises used to develop your résumé. Describing your accomplishments in the language employers use to describe the value they look for in candidates is a good strategy to begin the process of building an effective online résumé.

FACEBOOK

Facebook has emerged as the foremost social-networking site. Started in 2004 by three Harvard University students, the current version of Facebook remains true to its original purposes: to put people in touch with one another, share photos, and make it easy to meet new people. Like LinkedIn and other social-networking sites, you join by creating a profile, at which time you can browse and find others you know who also have Facebook accounts (those you went to school with, hometown affiliations, specialty interest groups, etc.). You can also let Facebook comb your current list of e-mail contacts, previous and current employers, and so on for current and former colleagues and coworkers. Many users search for specific people by individual names. Facebook has three levels of privacy controls that limit what others see, protecting you from unwanted persons.

The profile you create is called your Facebook Page, and that is what others see when they look you up on the Internet. It contains a space where you can upload a photo of yourself; a friends section that displays pictures of those you have befriended; a personal-information section of things you choose to share with other members; a mini-feed section that shares with others what you have been up to lately; and a section called the Wall, where others can leave messages, photos, Web links, and other things. Danger! Don't allow people to post inappropriate materials to your Facebook account. It is a good way to tarnish your brand and/or otherwise become disqualified for consideration for employment.

At this point, you are just getting started. Facebook accommodates applications that have been a continuing source of innovation and customization for users.

Some of the more prominent applications include photos, videos, groups, events, a marketplace (much like Craigslist), posted items, and virtual gifts. Facebook has been very aggressive in encouraging members to create their own applications and have added the Facebook developer application to assist. Another feature called Facebook Mobile allows users to access Facebook through mobile devices (cell phones and other PDAs), upload photos and videos, write status updates, comment on other users' photos and videos, write on other users' walls, and browse the site. And that is just the beginning.

Before discussing how to use Facebook in your job search, you need a basic understanding of Twitter because they are often used in combination with one another.

TWITTER

Twitter is one of the most interesting and innovative social-networking ideas to come along. A tweet is simply a message sent on Twitter. Texting and tweeting are actually one and the same, with one important difference: texting generally has one recipient in mind whereas tweeting can be broadcast to an entire network or a subset at once. This is not completely accurate but will do for purposes at present. As you get more familiar with texting and tweeting, the differences and similarities will become clearer.

Anyone can "tweet" by opening a free account. To reach other users you have to develop a network of contacts with Twitter accounts, as with other websites. However, Twitter has several limitations, including (1) phone-to-phone messages are limited to 140 characters, even though fuller text can be read by using a third-party developer desktop and Web-based applications; and (2) you can only send text—no photos or videos unless you use a third-party application. On the other hand, Twitter allows third-party developers partial access to its applications programs interface (API). Users have been very creative in the applications they have developed, including programs that use Twitter to send tweets through desktop applications and e-mail programs; search public tweets and coordinate with Google Maps to watch public tweets live throughout the world; and integrate with Facebook and other social-networking sites, including LinkedIn. The two most obvious uses of Twitter are individuals and groups that want to keep an audience of followers in the loop as things are happening, and those who want to follow such individuals and groups. Various combinations exist in between.

A Job-Search Example

All of this information is very interesting, you're probably saying, but how will it help me find a job? Let's take an example. Three months before the birth of her first child, Monica was notified that her job had been eliminated and that she would be eligible for a limited severance package. Her initial plans were to take short-term disability and a month's worth of unpaid family leave, and then return to work to uphold her end of the two-income standard of living she and her husband had enjoyed for the first four years of their marriage. They quickly decided to keep their initial plans intact as much as possible but include a search for a new position.

Monica's job-search strategy started with a target list of local companies that might be interested in someone with her credentials—an MBA in marketing, three years' experience with a Fortune 500 company, and a solid track record of project management. Timing was important, as her search had components that were both inactive and active—inactive before the baby was born and active once she was back on her feet and able to interview. Here is how each social-networking site was used.

Facebook fan pages for targeted companies were identified, and she signed up to be a "fan" in order to receive up-to-date information on available jobs and other current information. Three weeks before she was ready to interview, she let her network (mostly Facebook) know of her job situation and asked for leads, contacts, and referrals that might help. Several in her network knew of her situation and had asked if they could help before the baby was born. She requested that they hold off until she was closer to reentering the job market. This activity produced five leads for local jobs that had not yet been advertised or posted.

LinkedIn groups led her to undergraduate and graduate alumni associations, which she joined. Quiet moments at home during her pregnancy and later with the baby gave her time to connect online with other mothers looking to return to work. This also led to several leads that she "linked" to because she was able to identify contacts who were one, two, and three degrees of separation from her target companies.

Once the interviewing process started, Monica provided daily updates on what was happening through Twitter. One contact who had "retweeted" her tweets (i.e., sent them to a wider circle of friends) suggested other mothers who would be interested in keeping up with how to manage a job search, a pregnancy, and the birth of a child all at once. Still others were interested in the broader question of reentering the workforce. Monica briefly entertained the idea of starting a blog but did not get very far because she found a new position before her "unpaid" leave time ended. Once you start using social networks, you will quickly discover that Monica could have pursued many other avenues as well. But they were not necessary. Her endgame was a new job—and she got one.

▶ ▶ ▶

A word of caution: Much of what is suggested here involves the extensive use of computers, phones, and other technology-based equipment. This can be a double-edged sword. Companies have established the right to review the usage employees make of company-owned equipment. If you are at all concerned about keeping your job search private, use your own personal equipment—phone, computer, and so on. And advise potential employers to contact you away from work, on your privately owned equipment.

• • • • • • • • • **Things to Remember** • • • • • • • •

▶ *The work you did in preparing your résumé put your job search on solid footing. It provided you with a context for your previous accomplishments and helped you develop a résumé that featured what others view as important.*

▶ *Traditional advice that the job market is hidden is not valid. In truth, the job market is more splintered than hidden, and an emerging consensus among employers about the best place to look for talent situates the Internet as a core source.*

▶ *Know where to look for jobs, but that should not dictate how you look. How you go about a job search needs to be determined by where you are on the JS Pyramid in each particular job situation.*

▶ *Social networking has relegated face-to-face networking to being an appendage to what can be accomplished on the computer, not a substitute for it.*

▶ *The best way to learn about social networking is to get started by visiting and joining LinkedIn, Facebook, and Twitter.*

NOTES

1. Mark Granovetter, "The Strength of Weak Ties," *American Journal of Sociology* 78 (6): 1360–80.

2. Jerry Crispin and Mark Mehler, "CareerXroads Annual Source of Hire Study: Meltdown in 2009 and What It Means for a 2010 Recovery," www.careerxroads .com, accessed February 2010.

3. See "Closing the Employee Performance Gap—Boosting Competitiveness & Profit." Updated for EzineArticles (http://ezinearticles.com/?Closing-the-Employee-Performance-Gap---Boosting-Competitiveness-and-Profit&id= 3245235), November 13, 2009.

4. Crispin and Mehler, "CareerXroads."

5. Jerry Garfunkel, "The Digital Divide Between Age Groups," www.jerome.garfunkel .com, accessed June 30, 2005.

6. "Burson-Marsteller and Proof Digital Fortune 100 Social Media Study," July 31 2009, www.burson-marsteller.com/Innovation_and_insights/blogs_and_podcasts/ BM_Blog/Lists/Posts/Post.aspx?ID=128.

7. Crispin and Mehler, "CareerXroads."

8. Charlene Li and Josh Bernoff, *Groundswell: Winning in a World Transformed by Social Technologies* (Cambridge, Mass.: Harvard Business School Publishing, 2008).

R U L E #4

Interviews: They're About the Value You Demonstrate

THE NEXT STEP in getting your job requires that you ace those interviews. Being invited for an interview is good news because it means you have moved to a higher rung on the Job-Search Pyramid, which was shown in Figure 3.1. You have piqued the interest of the hiring organization, and it is willing to explore your credentials further. Congratulations! In this era of supercompetition among white-collar workers, you have put your best foot forward. But you will need to do it again during the interview process.

You will likely have to interview with more than one person, and possibly go through several rounds, before a decision is made. Companies know how important selecting a new hire is and that the process is more art than science. Several key people may want to size up the applicants, which is why the multiple rounds of interviewing are used to whittle the pile down to the final candidate. Even then, you may be invited to another round as a final check—just to make sure they have made the right choice. Don't be surprised if along the way you are also asked to take a written assessment test. There are tests that measure everything from aptitude to personality, and companies use them often.

Before you run the gauntlet, however, you should understand what hiring organizations are trying to accomplish when they interview candidates. Here again, the process is not about you. The companies want certain attributes in the person they hire, and they try to determine which of the candidates will most likely deliver for them. At the end of the day, they make their best guesstimate of who can provide the most value at the price they are willing to pay. Your job is to convince them that that person is you.

Be Relaxed and Be Prepared: The Job Interviewee's Motto

An interview is a form of examination. Employers test candidates to see which one best meets their needs. Experts on testing agree that to achieve your maximum performance, you must relax. That is, you should go into interviews with an uncluttered mind. This advice is given for every kind of test, from driver's licenses to college entrance exams to employment tests.

How do you relax? One of the keys to relaxation is feeling the comfort that comes from being well prepared. Solid preparation breeds the confidence that you will perform at your highest level. It also helps you be flexible so that you can answer any type of question thrown your way.

For example, Gail was midway through a daylong set of interviews before she realized a major flaw in her preparation. The interviewers' questions were unexpectedly negative. "What have you failed at in your career and why?" "What kind of people do you least like working with?" "What is the best way to fire someone?" After a while she could not remember what answers she gave or whom she gave them to. Her prep time had been spent reading books on interviewing and memorizing what the authors promised would be "winning answers to tough interview questions." Yet her rehearsed answers felt disconnected from her personal experiences. "There has to be a better way," she thought.

You can divide the preparation for interviews into three categories: interview protocols (accepted etiquette), structures (the different kinds of interviews you are likely to encounter), and content (the questions themselves). Preparation for the first two types requires minimum memorization. The third takes advantage of the work you did when you developed your résumé and saw yourself in terms of the value you create. But let's examine each of these types in turn.

Protocols: Accepted Etiquette

This section covers some rules of the road that most companies abide by and contains helpful hints that are easy to remember. Now is also a good time to clear up some common misconceptions.

BE ON TIME

Sometimes people are confused about what "on time" means. The safe answer is that being on time means getting to the interview somewhere between fifteen minutes and an hour before the interview is to start. You may intuitively sense that showing up an hour early is inappropriate and potentially awkward. For instance, you could accidentally bump into candidates who have been scheduled ahead of you, with appointment spacing far enough apart to avoid chance meetings. Similarly, you risk having the normal operations of the office conducted around you, as you sit and wait for an extended time. Arriving too early also gives you too much time to kill, especially if the interview starts late. That extra waiting time will likely heighten your anxiety. Yet you don't want to cut it too close or you'll risk being late.

Confused? Don't be. "On time" means more than one thing. In one sense, it is the time you need to be available to the interviewers. In another sense, it is the time you should be near the facility but beyond the immediate physical environment of the interview location.

Barney had to rush to catch a taxi and, upon arrival, he made a mad dash up two flights of stairs to be "on time" for his 2:00 interview. He made it with three minutes to spare—or did he? A normal level of pre-interview anxiety and the summer heat combined to produce a shower of sweat dripping from his face during the entire interview. His careful preparation evaporated in the swelter of physical discomfort. He was on time but too late to interview effectively.

Take the time before the interview starts to get the physical lay of the land and do last-minute preparation, such as reviewing your notes and making sure your cell phone is turned off. Under these more relaxed circumstances you can plan your arrival to the general vicinity of the facility, beyond the immediate physical environment of the interview and up to as much as an hour ahead. Then, be at the interview location about fifteen minutes before the interview is scheduled to begin. Of course, that brief time should be adjusted if you have been told to arrive early to fill out paperwork. If the interview is located in another city or is in an unfamiliar part of town, you may want to make a dry run to the interview site the day before.

APPROPRIATE ATTIRE

What to wear? Dress guidelines for an interview vary slightly for men and women. Men have fewer choices—generally, a dark business suit, a white long-sleeve shirt, a color-coordinated tie, black socks, and black lace-up dress shoes. Modest variations to this standard are generally acceptable (e.g., blue shirt and dark loafers) but are less safe. It is, of course, possible to show your personality or fashion sense and still be appropriate. That could be something as small as the color of your tie or even the type of knot. But the advisability of this depends on the industry—some corporate settings are more rigid or conservative than others. Generally, self-expression is welcomed in less conservative industries. The best approach is to consult someone in human resources for advice on what is appropriate. When in doubt, however, it is better to be too conservative than too casual.

Other grooming tips include being clean shaven or with neatly trimmed facial hair (no facial hair is the safest), having neatly groomed hair, and wearing no flashy jewelry or loud cologne. If you visit any reputable men's clothing store, you'll get good advice about what to wear. If you are shopping, tell the salesperson you need a suit and coordinating components for a job interview, and the sales associate will help you pick an appropriate wardrobe.

For women, whose choices are broader, a dark business suit (with knee-length skirt) usually works best. Hair should be worn off the face and neatly pinned, as needed. An interview is neither the time nor the place for frilly blouses or a display of cleavage. As with men, skin-piercing decorations, save for modest earrings, are no-no's. Strong perfume or cologne is also to be avoided.

Finding the appropriate dress for an interview is tricky because we are a diverse society, with different cultural and religious norms. If your clothing and grooming habits differ from generally accepted norms, check with the company so personnel will not be surprised by your appearance—at least they can communicate what they understand to be acceptable. If you already have multiple piercings of the ear or other visible parts of your body and/or tattoos, you may want to dress in a way that does not draw attention to them. Remove any adorning jewelry and cover tattoos, if possible.

What should you do if a company's official dress code is business casual or less? You will, from time to time, encounter this situation, as Bill did when he interviewed to be a project leader at a Silicon Valley company. When asked, the recruiting manager and search consultant told him that business suits were specifically forbidden, and that the company's president and all the others he would meet would be wearing blue jeans. High-tech companies in particular often go to considerable lengths to create informal work environments at every level in the organization, and this also applies to visitors. And these companies are not shy about informing visitors about their dress code. Most companies have not gone that casual, but many do allow employees to come to work dressed "business casual."

So what does "business casual" mean? Claudia thought she covered the subject when she asked a representative from HR what the company's dress code was. "Business casual," he said. She ended up inappropriately dressed for her interview. A better approach would have been to inform HR how she intended to dress and get a specific sign-off on that. "I understand your work attire is business casual. Is that the expectation for those coming in for interviews?" Absent more specific information, play it safe and dress in the more formal business style.

Also, remember that companies mean dramatically different things by "business casual"—it can be anything from dress slacks and sport jackets to blue jeans. At all times, however, it means crisp, neat, and appropriate, even for a chance meeting with company VIPs or the CEO. In any regard, avoid the extremes. You should not look as if you are headed for either a night at the opera or a day at the beach. Likewise, avoid the extremes of tight or baggy clothing. When you think about business casual, think classic rather than trendy.

On occasion, you may have a job interview after normal working hours. If the dress required for the interview is different from your current working environment's and you don't have time to change, different attire at work could be a telltale sign you're headed for an interview. Let the interviewer know how you will be dressed and why. The person will likely understand.

What about job fairs? Job fairs are an economical way for companies to search for talent, especially for entry-level white-collar positions. The expected attire is usually listed on the promotional materials accompanying the fair. When "business attire" is specified, the aforementioned guidelines should suffice. A "business casual" designation can, however, lead to all sorts of difficulties. Because recent graduates often go to job fairs, many college and university placement centers have published guidelines for students to follow. The one presented in Figure 4.1 is that offered by Career Services, at Virginia Tech University. (For any updated version for the dress code visit www.vatech.edu and search "business casual dress code.")

FIGURE 4.1 Business casual dress guidelines.

Business Casual Guidelines for Men and Women

Business casual is crisp, is neat, and should look appropriate even for a chance meeting with a CEO. It should not look like cocktail or party or picnic attire. Avoid tight or baggy clothing.

Basics: Khaki or dark pants, neatly pressed, and a pressed long-sleeved, buttoned solid shirt are safe for both men and women. Women can wear sweaters; cleavage is not business-appropriate (despite what you see in the media). Polo/golf shirts, unwrinkled, are an appropriate choice if you know the environment will be quite casual, outdoors, or in a very hot location. This may not seem like terribly exciting attire, but you are not trying to stand out for your cutting-edge look, but for your good judgment in a business environment.

Shoes/belt: Wear a leather belt and leather shoes. Athletic shoes are inappropriate.

Cost/quality: You are not expected to be able to afford the same clothing as a corporate CEO; however, do invest in the quality that will look appropriate during your first two or three years on the job for a business casual environment or occasions.

Details: Everything should be clean, well pressed, and not show wear. Even the nicest khakis after 100 washings may not be your best choice for a reception. Carefully inspect new clothes for tags, and all clothes for dangling threads, etc. (as with interview attire).

Use common sense: If there is six inches of snow on the ground and/or you are rushing to get to an information session between classes and you left home 12 hours earlier, no one will expect you to show up looking ready for a photo shoot—they'll just be happy you made it. Just avoid wearing your worst gym clothes and jeans. If you show up at an event and realize you're not as well dressed as you should be, make a quick, pleasant apology and make a good impression with your interpersonal skills and intelligent questions.

SPECIFICS FOR MEN'S BUSINESS CASUAL

Ties: Ties are generally not necessary for business casual, but if you are in doubt, you can wear a tie. It never hurts to slightly overdress; by dressing nicely, you pay a compliment to your host. You can always wear the tie and discreetly walk by the room where the function is held; if no one else is wearing a tie, you can discreetly remove yours.

Shirts: Long-sleeved shirts are considered dressier than short-sleeved and are appropriate even in summer. Choosing white or light blue solid, or conservative stripes is your safest bet. Polo shirts (tucked in, of course) are acceptable in more casual situations.

Socks: Wear dark socks, mid-calf length so no skin is visible when you sit down.

Shoes: Leather shoes should be worn. No sandals, athletic shoes, or hiking boots.

Facial hair: Just as with an interview: Facial hair, if worn, should be well groomed. Know your industry and how conservative it is; observe men in your industry if you are unsure what's appropriate or are considering changing your look.

Jewelry: Wear a conservative watch. If you choose to wear other jewelry, be conservative. Removing earrings is safest. For conservative industries, don't wear earrings. Observe other men in your industry to see what is acceptable.

SPECIFICS FOR WOMEN'S BUSINESS CASUAL

Don't confuse club attire with business attire. If you would wear it to a club, you probably shouldn't wear it in a business environment. Also, most attire worn on television is not appropriate for business environments. Don't be deluded.

WHAT TO TAKE TO AN INTERVIEW

Keep it simple. You've been called to the interview and your desired impression is of an organized, streamlined person. Trying to quickly retrieve what you need from a cluttered briefcase filled with papers is awkward. Rustling through loose papers gives the appearance of disorganization and forgetfulness.

Start with a black leather portfolio binder; a pad of lined notepaper; two ballpoint pens (in case one fails); a schedule of whom you are to meet and their titles; your notes; a list of references; extra copies of your résumé; and business cards, if appropriate. Using business cards can be tricky if your current employer doesn't know you are interviewing, or if the information on the card is no longer accurate—that is, you no longer work at the address listed on the card. People generally understand if you tell them to contact you at work "with discretion." Remember, if you are using a company phone, or computer, some employers track Internet and phone usage. In fact, having old business cards is a constant reminder that you are between jobs. If you are just starting out in your career, nobody will expect you to have a business card. Allow the contact information on your résumé to suffice.

If you decide to take more items to your interview, use a briefcase. But don't use the extra space as an invitation to add clutter.

YOUR LIST OF REFERENCES

You should have your list of references available at the interview, even though you will usually be allowed additional time to submit them. If it is too early in the process, you may not be asked. But having such a list handy shows organization and forethought.

Sometimes companies will specify that they want references from those who have played particular roles in your professional life—supervisor(s), colleagues, and the like. When particulars are not specified, the most desirable references include your direct supervisors, clients, colleagues, and subordinates—all people who will have firsthand knowledge of your work.

Students preparing for an interview have roughly the same priority order, but with a little more flexibility. For example, deans and other university officials with whom you may not have worked directly or had only limited contact can be valuable additions to a list of references. The same is true for parents of roommates and other college-related acquaintances. However, references from your parents or from other kinship relations won't help your cause and are considered inappropriate.

Reference checkers fully understand that you will ask for references only from those you trust will give you positive recommendations. That is why a negative or even a lukewarm recommendation quickly becomes a red flag that could signal problems and destroy your chances of getting the job. Be sure you get permission from people ahead of time before adding them to your list, and make sure they are willing to give you a positive recommendation. Don't be afraid to ask them directly, "I am in the process of applying for jobs at a number of companies and was wondering if you are in a position to give me a strong recommendation?" If they are willing but you sense hesitation, accept the offer to help but think twice about adding them to your final list.

You should also let your references know that you will use them only when you are a serious candidate for a position. Companies do not enjoy reference checking and will do it only for those candidates who are on the short list. However, it has become common practice to check candidates' online profiles (Facebook, Twitter, LinkedIn, etc.) at the very beginning of the interview process.

Otherwise, when the company checks your references, take that as a strong signal you have made the final list and a job offer could be forthcoming, although there are exceptions. For example, Teach for America requires reference letters for candidates before they are invited for interviews. From there, it is still a steep climb to a final offer. Regardless, a request for references indicates that you have moved up the Job-Search Pyramid, and your chances of acceptance have improved accordingly.

COACH YOUR REFERENCES

Don't be shy about coaching your references on what to say. Return to the exercises you used to prepare your résumé. Here is another opportunity to put value creation to work on your behalf. The match between your value-infused accomplishment statements and the position description will likely tell you what the hiring organization wants to hear from a reference. For example, if the position calls for someone with strong project-management skills, leadership, and/or political savvy, you should coach your references to comment about your strengths in those areas as they experienced them.

Especially, be sure to thank your references for their help at the same time as you prompt them. A typical note from you might read: "Thanks for serving as a reference. I understand they are particularly interested in strong leaders with good project-management skills—you know, someone who has the political savvy to get things done. Any comments you could make about these would be helpful. Also, let me know if you need additional information about what I have accomplished in these areas."

Additionally, encourage your references to use the language companies use when they describe the characteristics they are looking for in the candidates. That is the value they look to create, and your references can help you greatly if they describe your strengths in those terms.

OBTAIN SECONDARY REFERENCES

Staffing pros know that the deck is stacked against finding out anything of significance from references that are volunteered by the candidates. Candid references are hard to come by. Consequently, they rely on secondary references to provide more accurate assessments. These are often found through the initial list you provide. After the call to a reference has been completed, an interviewer may ask, "Are there other people you know who might be familiar with his [her] work?" It does not happen often, but it is a good possibility and you want to be aware of and deal with this possibility ahead of time if you think it is appropriate.

One way to accomplish this is to provide your references with a secondary list in the event they are asked. These people should be treated the same as those on your primary list. That is, you get their permission, you make sure they are able to give you a strong reference, and you coach them to cover things of value to the hiring organization. Don't delineate the two lists for your references or the company. Do not refer to them as "primary" and "secondary," or even mark them with an "A" or a "B." Just tell all your references that they will be contacted only for positions for which you are a serious candidate. It is okay to refer to your secondary list as "Additional References."

The header for your list of references is usually the same as the header for your résumé except that it specifies that what comes below are "Personal References."

MICHELLE STREET, CPA
9501 Any Street
Chicago, Illinois 60600
312-555-0000
michelle@buzztech.com

Personal References

The contact information for each reference should be formatted as follows:

Mr. Paul Neumann
Director, Financial Analysis
IBM
123 Big Blue Drive

Ossining, New York 12345
(555) 555-5555
Former Supervisor

Notice that the e-mail address is not included. Safety walls will sometimes make it difficult for outsiders to connect with your references if they have not previously exchanged e-mails. That is, company spam filters often do not allow these e-mails through to the intended recipient. Check with each of your references to see if that is the case. If not, include their e-mail addresses on your reference list.

FOLLOW-UP THANK YOU

You should follow up every interview with written correspondence to the hiring manager and/or whoever formally represented the company during the interview process. Differences of opinion exist on the way to do this, varying from formal written letters to e-mails and even handwritten notes. The main point is that the medium used is less important than the content and intent. The purpose of follow-up communication is to thank company representatives for their time, confirm the next steps and time frames, review any points that need to be emphasized, and deliver on commitments made during the interview.

The sample follow-up letter in Figure 4.2 is in the format of a formal typewritten letter and contains all of these elements. If the company's culture accepts e-mails as formal communications (many do), then an e-mail response will suffice. If you are unsure, however, a formal typewritten letter is the safest approach. Handwritten notes are generally not recommended, but it is up to you. Sometimes a handwritten note to a "behind-the-scenes" coordinator is a nice touch and contributes to the overall positive impression. This can also be an effective way to stand out at job fairs, where company recruiters meet as many as 100 different candidates.

Structure: Interviews, Tests, Tours

Your objective in each interview situation is the same: to stand out. If you are an effective listener, your chances are greatly improved. However, listening is hard work, and not everyone knows how to do it effectively. The best technique is to listen to the interviewer's question all the way through, pause briefly, and articulate an

FIGURE 4.2 Sample follow-up letter.

Michelle Street
9501 Any Street
Chicago, IL 60600

Mr. John Wayne
Vice President, Financial Planning
ACME Corp.
1111 A Street
New York, NY 00000

March 12, 2011

Dear John:

I just wanted to drop a quick note to thank you and your team for the opportunity to interview with ACME. The position sounds interesting and is very much in line with my career interest and ambition.

During the course of the interview a question came up as to whether the position is large enough in scope to hold my attention for an extended period of time. I think there is plenty to learn and would have no reason to try to rush to another assignment. My commitment will be to add value for as long as possible in any assignment I have. If you have questions about this, or other aspects of the interview, please feel free to contact me. I would be pleased to continue our discussion.

I understand you will finish interviewing next week and anticipate a final decision shortly thereafter. I will touch base with you the week of April 5 to see if the process is still on track.

Again, thank you for your time and interest.

Regards,

Michelle Street

answer. Far too many people start formulating an answer before the interviewer has finished asking the question. It is as if they are afraid there will be a moment of silence during the course of the interview.

Impatience creates problems that do not help your candidacy. First, you may rush forward with half-baked answers that do not respond to the intent of the question. Poor listeners also give the appearance of not being able to understand the question. There is a difference between offering assured answers that demonstrate command of the subject and shooting from the hip. Finally, some interview situations absolutely demand that you listen to the entirety of what is being asked before responding (video interviews are an example). You must incorporate good listening habits into your overall approach to interviewing.

Here is a practice tip. The next time you are among friends (perhaps giving someone an update on your job search), practice listening to each of their questions through to the end, pause for a moment to think about what you want to say, and say it. You will likely have a smoother, more fully satisfying conversation than normal. When you listen to questions all the way through, you will discover that many of them were asked rhetorically—that is, the listener sees the answer as self-evident. It is important to avoid trying to answer rhetorical questions, and the best way to do that is to listen to the entire question. This simple exercise will help you make your answers more organized, concise, and on target—all desirable outcomes in an interview.

Interviews can be structured in several ways, and you have to perform well in all of them. Kara expected that her day of interviews would feature a series of traditional one-on-one conversations. She knew several other candidates were interviewing that day, but she never thought they would be brought together for a group session that pitted them against one another. Totally surprised, she could not help showing her dismay about the situation, and she performed poorly in the balance of the one-on-one interviews. When you are preparing for an interview, expect the unexpected. Your familiarity with the different types of interviews can help you manage the unexpected.

The types of interviews mentioned here represent the vast majority of types you are likely to encounter. The message is, do not be surprised by the different ways you may be assessed, always be on guard, and go with the flow.

TRADITIONAL ONE-ON-ONE INTERVIEWS

The interviews you are most likely to encounter will be one-on-one conversations. In fact, an entire day can be taken up with speaking to various company representatives about the job opening. Don't be surprised if the first interview is with someone from human resources whose sole responsibility is to determine if you should be passed forward to others that day or not. When candidates come across as particularly well suited for the opening, they can be passed forward to other interviewers right away (very often to those who can make immediate hiring decisions). Other times, there will be a series of interviews, beginning with the initial screening. Companies use this screening method to avoid wasting management time with candidates who obviously won't work out. Why should a company schedule a full slate of interviews for candidates who will not make it through the first round?

Interviews with multiple interviewers sometimes are opportunities for the company to screen successively for different things, including technical competence, organizational fit, background, familiarity with industry issues, and even overall likeability. The initial care you took to develop a focused résumé that linked your past accomplishments to a company's needs pays additional dividends at this point. You are well prepared and you understand how your experiences fit with the value being sought by the company. You just need to present that value in a calm, collected manner.

INTERVIEWS OVER DINNER OR LUNCH

This is not a time to relax. Even over a meal, you are still in an interview situation. Companies often want to know how you act in social settings. Pay attention, listen, and follow the lead of your host, especially when it comes to alcohol consumption. For lunch, you should avoid alcohol altogether, even if your host chooses to imbibe.

The situation is slightly different for dinner. Follow the lead of your host by consuming alcohol only if he or she does. If your table of interviewers makes split decisions (some do and others don't), you should abstain. You want to continue to concentrate on the questions asked, hear them all the way through, and formulate thoughtful answers. That works best when you are as sober as the person asking the question. If you do drink, try to stick with wine and a maximum of two servings.

By the way, don't be overly concerned if you are dining at a formal restaurant with more knives and forks than you know what to do with. Most likely, the others are not sure, either. Generally, the way utensils are laid out intends that you use the outermost fork or spoon with each course, and proceed in toward the plate as each course is offered.

PRESENTATION INTERVIEWS

More common in academic settings or where intellectual property is an important part of the product the company or department produces, the presentation interview can be an ideal situation because (theoretically, at least) you are in charge of what you want to say. On the flip side, such an interview can be difficult if someone in the audience is hostile to your candidacy or insists on interrupting in a way that disturbs the flow of the points you want to make.

The best tactic for this interview type is to encourage interruptions and simultaneously explain, "I prefer that we cover things you are interested in rather than get through my presentation." Most audiences will understand when interruptions are unreasonable and will side with the presenter.

GROUP COMPETITIONS

Companies sometimes organize a group session as a way to measure individuals' performance under pressure. Usually, a group of candidates is given conflicting objectives, such as "win the group over to your particular point of view but help the group come to a decision within a specified time frame." The advice is to play it straight. Make contributions to the group as you can, explain your point of view clearly, and do not force the issue. Dominating the group to the detriment of others or to the group as a whole is not the right approach, nor is failing to make any contribution at all.

GOOD COP/BAD COP INTERVIEWS

Some interview situations are intentionally structured to see how you react under a different kind of pressure. Sometimes an interviewer will be hostile and aggressive toward you. For example, you might hear:

> ▶ "Not sure why you came all the way for this interview. I hear the job's already been filled."

‣ "That last answer of yours was the worst I have ever heard."

At other times, more than one interviewer at a time is involved (usually two), in which one is hostile and the other is accommodating to see if they can goad you into inappropriate behavior, especially when the "bad cop" leaves the room. Generally speaking, you should underreact. That is, do not return the hostility or forget that you must do well on the interview, regardless of what new information is received or the demeanor of the interviewers.

TELEPHONE INTERVIEWS

The telephone is used most frequently to screen applicants before going to the expense of inviting them in for additional consideration. Still, congratulations are in order here because you have undoubtedly advanced further than many other candidates. The one major disadvantage of a telephone interview is that you do not receive feedback from the interviewer's body language to help you interpret the situation. Careful listening becomes even more important.

For such an interview, choose a private room (at home, if possible) away from background noise and interruptions. The rules about clutter still apply. If your phone has a high-quality speaker, use it so your hands are free to take notes and retrieve documents as they are needed. The same is true if you are using a cell phone with a headset. However, when the call is first initiated, you should not use the speaker feature until you have received permission from the interviewer to do so. You can ask, "I would like to have my hands free to take notes. Do you mind if I put you on the speakerphone?"

VIDEO INTERVIEWS

Video interviews can be tricky because of the delay between the audio and video displays. If one participant does not wait until the other is done talking before responding, it throws the entire interview off, and it has the effect of people's stepping on one another's conversations. Waiting until the other person is finished speaking before answering usually avoids this problem. Also, be sure your surrounding environment is neat and uncluttered, and look directly into the camera when speaking. Dress as if the interview is being conducted in person.

OTHER INTERVIEW TYPES: ASSESSMENT TESTS, COMPANY TOURS, PANELS

Candidates may be asked to take an assessment test as part of the interview process. Some tests measure personality characteristics to determine if you will fit with the culture. An alternative test is a skills/intelligence tool that measures your ability to learn. You should play it straight and not try to "psych" the tests out. Answer the questions honestly and do not give answers you think they are looking for. You either have what they are looking for or you do not. You too want to know that the situation is the right one.

Similarly, serious candidates may be given a grand tour of a facility to meet with various heads in groups, who will likely be asked to provide feedback before the final hiring decision is made. This is a bit of a beauty contest in which employees are given the opportunity to ask questions. In these situations, your listening skills are fully needed to pick up on any issues the questioners consider important. This is not the time for bold proclamations or idle promises. A simple acknowledgment of the issues raised and a commitment to be responsive are usually sufficient.

In a variation of the grand tour, you may be interviewed by a panel. If possible, find out ahead of time who the panel members are, what roles they play, and what issues are important to them. You may want to jot their names down in order of how the panel is arrayed around the table. It will help you recall their names as you respond to various questions.

Content: Interview Questions

Interviewing is more art than science. The overwhelming number of interviews you participate in will not be conducted by highly trained experts. Even staffing professionals who fill positions for a living seldom have enough training to classify as expert interviewers.

Don't think, however, that they do not know what they are doing. The lack of expertise simply means they don't use the data taken from interviews to make scientifically valid distinctions between candidates. Savvy staffing professionals know that the impressions they get from interviews need to be verified in other ways. Much of the data garnered from interviews is used to eliminate people rather than to verify whether they are best for the job at hand. Interviewers are assessing such qualities as listening skills, general appearance, and one's level of personal organization—all factors you should be able to handle if you have followed our advice.

Given the interviewer's lack of interviewing expertise, don't think that all questions are equally focused on distinguishing one candidate from another. Some questions are simply icebreakers—a way of getting started with little, if any, evaluative meaning intended, such as, "How was your trip in?" "Before we start, do you have any questions about what we have planned today?" "Do you have any questions about the materials I e-mailed you?"

Nevertheless, all questions should be taken as opportunities to add to an overall impression that stands up well against other candidates. Don't engage in idle chatter about how you got lost on the way to the interview. If you need additional information, now is a good time to get it. If not, move on.

You should also be aware that some questions (more than interviewers like to admit) are just fillers. That is, they are asked for purposes of filling the time an interviewer has been given to complete the interview. These are largely unrelated to the information needed to make a hiring recommendation.

For every interview, however, there is a core group of questions that directly relate to determining if you are the right candidate for the job. These are the questions for which you must be prepared. For those who understand the principles of value creation, this is good news, on two counts. First, all the answers to these questions are the same, in that they are opportunities to talk about things of value to the employer. Second, you have already learned what those valued things are and have the language to describe them; you did this when you focused your résumé on the job at hand. But let's return to those exercises and use them to prepare for the interview.

GENERAL INTERVIEW PREPARATION

Above all else, avoid overdoing your preparation. Do not try to be ready for every possible question you could be asked. An interview is not an exercise in rote memorization. If you treat it as such, you will likely come across as stiff and mechanical in your answers. You also stand a good chance of being unable to recall details on demand.

Your answers to questions need to reflect your own experiences and not be fabricated. Besides moral considerations, the truth is always easier to remember than a lie. In addition, when you tell the truth, the weight of being ethical is on your side. Similarly, interviewing is like most things in life: the more practice you have, the better you will become. Once you have experience interviewing, the answers will flow naturally and you will find the comfort and relaxation that comes with being well prepared.

Remember that jobs in the same industry or function have a certain degree of overlap. Preparing for one job interview goes a long way toward preparing for others. That is why, to gain experience, you should sometimes interview for jobs even if you suspect you will not become a final candidate or accept an offer.

SPECIFIC INTERVIEW PREPARATION

The best preparation for an interview involves three steps: (1) visit what a company is trying to accomplish when filling the job for which you are applying, (2) match your background against its interests, and (3) align your experiences to answer potentially difficult questions.

An interview is a test in which you demonstrate the relevance of your résumé to the job. Interviewers want to know what you have done and whether you can perform with distinction. Though there are many average performers, no company intentionally fills a position expecting average performance. The distinctions between candidates are based largely on price and performance expectations. Your chances of being noticed are improved if your résumé is written using the same language the company uses to describe the value it wants in filling the position. That is, an interview is an attempt to confirm that what's on paper will be reflected in your performance on the job. Preparation for an interview should focus on the links between the experiences captured in your résumé and the expectations of the job. You can accomplish this in three relatively easy steps, as mentioned above.

QUESTIONS OF RELEVANT EXPERIENCE If you have been through interviews before, you may have noticed that interviewers have a copy of your résumé in front of them and they use it to structure the interview. A typical question might be: "I noticed that you were a project manager for ACME for five years. Tell me about that experience." How do you answer this question?

First, listen to the question all the way through, pause, and formulate an answer. The answers to all interview questions should be regarded as opportunities to talk about things of interest to the interviewer. For example, if the position description calls for "strong project-management skills with a minimum of five years' experience," your answer might be as follows: "That's where I developed strength in the area. A couple of projects in particular were important steps along the way. . . ." Recall projects that were particularly challenging and describe the required additional skills, including leadership and political savvy.

Once you create the connection between your accomplishments and their interests, you will be able to bring these to life in the stories you tell about past jobs. These stories, though, should reflect what you have actually accomplished. They will be easier to remember and will stand the test of reference checking.

But what if the position description did not mention project-management skills? Suppose the question catches you by surprise? Relax and give a straightforward answer to the best of your ability. If project management is a subject you are uncomfortable discussing, ask for further clarification from the interviewer, such as, "What aspect of project management would you like me to speak to?"

At first, interview preparation may feel a little awkward. But you will get the hang of it quickly, especially when you use your alignment sheets as a guide rather than trying to commit them to memory. Your familiarity with the links between your background and their requirements can give you a substantial edge over other candidates. And the more you prepare, the more you can relax and perform at your highest level.

Let's revisit the "key word" exercise and resume the examples of Michelle Street used in Chapter 2. Figure 4.3 lists ACME's key words.

Michelle's experiences in her accomplishment statements line up as indicated in Figure 4.4.

Again, notice the italicized portions of the accomplishment statements as they represent the use of key words to describe what the candidate has done. However, you should not try to force all questions to fit into your alignment. Interviewers are notorious for wandering off in directions unrelated to the task

FIGURE 4.3 Key words from ACME Bank position description.

ACME Bank is an integrated financial services organization providing personal, business, corporate, and institutional clients with banking, lending, investing, and financial management solutions. We are deeply committed to a high-performance culture, one that values diversity, continuous learning, employee commitment, and community involvement.

We reward our talented professionals with a base salary and competitive compensation package, life, health, dental, pension plan, 401(k), and an exceptional working environment.

SPECIFIC ACCOUNTABILITIES
Strategy
Understanding the corporate initiatives of the Bank, participate in or develop future-oriented strategies to maximize shareholder value as required

▶ Partner with clients to develop future-oriented strategies to maximize shareholder value.

Advisory
▶ Provide consulting and support to customers by continually offering value-added ideas, advice, and solutions.

▶ Work in partnership with the client to assist in optimal structuring of new initiatives and strategies. Ensure that structures comply with regulatory rules and guidelines.

▶ Work as a valued business partner to develop, implement, and track value-maximizing strategies—business planning, forecasting, and reporting on results.

▶ Provide financial advice to clients on impacts of various business transactions (investments/divestitures, securitizations, etc.).

Governance and Analysis/Results
▶ Provide weekly, monthly, quarterly, and annual reports as required.

▶ Prepare both formal and informal reports and analysis for the client as required to support strategic objectives, decision making, and solution resolution.

▶ Responsible for ensuring that risks are identified and mitigated.

▶ Coordinate the annual planning processes.

▶ Review and provide financial concurrence related to the approval of a capital expenditure.

▶ Attest as required to LOB's compliance with applicable policies, including corporate policies and accounting policies. Provide input and concurrence to new policies impacting LOB.

Support
▶ Lead or participate in project teams as required for new initiatives, process improvements, or technology implementation and development.

▶ Provide leadership by recruiting, developing, and maintaining high-quality staff, and ensuring that processes are in place to do this.

(continued)

▶ Responsible for staff training and development.

▶ Responsible for providing ongoing feedback on performance and ensuring timely completion of annual review process.

▶ Ensure that skill levels remain commensurate with the requirements of the position. Responsible for identifying skills gaps and taking appropriate actions to close those gaps.

▶ Key contacts: LOB and Group executives, Controllers Bank of Montreal Group of Companies, Finance departments.

▶ Internal/external auditors, Regulatory agencies VBM.

▶ Support VBM initiatives by understanding VBM metrics, providing financial information, and performing VBM-based analysis as required.

Knowledge & Skills

▶ CPA or degree in Accounting/Finance

▶ 6–8 years of work experience in a financial services environment

▶ Knowledge of banking structures

▶ Strong interpersonal, verbal, and written communication skills

▶ Experience in preparing and delivering presentations

▶ Experience in planning, forecasting, and analysis

▶ Project, process, and change management skills

▶ Good working knowledge of LAN-based software programs including Word, Excel, PowerPoint

To explore this opportunity to join ACME Bank, visit our website and apply for position Job ID 55555 at www.acmebank.com.

---

at hand. Your job is to recognize every opportunity to demonstrate that you are the best candidate for the job. And you accomplish that by good answers to the pertinent questions.

QUESTIONS OF SHORTCOMINGS AND FAILURE You prep for tough questions a little differently because the wrong answer can have disastrous consequences. However, let's be clear about what we mean by "tough." A question that requires additional thought does not necessarily qualify as tough. For our purposes, a question is "tough" when a wrong answer can sink your candidacy. These are usually questions that attempt to solicit unprepared or spontaneous responses. If you are well prepared, they will be easy to handle. Yet giving a quick, unthinking

FIGURE 4.4 Examples of accomplishment statements.

Employer	Dates	Position	Accomplishment Statements
Big Service Firm	2002–2004	Director of Finance, US Commercial Operations	• Proposed and led the development of the revenue planning tool *that increased sales force and finance team productivity 65 percent while increasing revenue forecasting accuracy, then organized and managed the consultant team that implemented the project.* Received the 2002 Award for Excellence for this effort. • Led negotiations for *data acquisition, licensing agreements, joint ventures, and organizational restructuring* that enabled the launch of a restructured US commercial organization *with optimal initiatives and strategies.* • Converted a group of diversified financial technicians using value-maximizing strategies into a high-performance global resource by setting high expectations for the department, training them in sophisticated new skills, and coaching each one on communication and presentation techniques.
Acme Marketing Company	1999–2002	Director, Global Business Analysis	• *Partnered with clients* to design and implement the new client revenue forecasting model and financial planning package across the company, *greatly improving the management team's ability to efficiently and effectively manage financial performance.* • Researched, analyzed, and presented all P&L and balance sheet forecasts in clear, concise form, projecting changes in revenue, operating income, debt levels, cash position, interest payments, and compensation calculations associated with acquisitions. • Created and produced the company's first comprehensive global strategic plan by *reengineering the process, standardizing the formats and reports, and leading the reviews with senior management and the executive board.*
Big Drug Company 1988–1999	1998–1999	Manager, Competitive Analysis and Forecasting, Medical Products Marketing	• Directed the commercial analysis and forecasting for the new development business units with annual sales exceeding $1 billion, while providing the competitive analysis activities for all business units in this $4 billion division. • Analyzed corporate initiatives and negotiated the proposal that led to a $50 million strategic alliance agreement between the company and an outside pharmaceutical company.

(continued)

Employer	Dates	Position	Accomplishment Statements
			‣ Created an in-depth analysis of a major therapeutic category and coordinated the proper launch positioning and resources that supported the product being licensed to launch in the US. The 2002 revenues for this product exceeded $400 million. ‣ Directed external consultant teams in developing actionable analyses on market and competitive developments by offering value-added ideas, advice, and solutions.
Big Drug Company 1988–1999	1996–1997	Associate Manager, Micromarketing, Medical Products Marketing	‣ Directed staff of eight financial and marketing professionals in physician targeting and analysis for the marketing and sales organizations with an emphasis on ROI for the $100 million promotions budget. ‣ Refocused the Internet promotion spending, improving communication to target audiences and saving $700,000 annually. ‣ Reengineered the promotions analysis process and vendor relationships, which cut the time of analysis turnaround from four weeks to one week while reducing analysis costs 70 percent. ‣ Integrated promotions planning tools into the market planning process, which provided high visibility of costs and maximized promotion spending ROI.
Big Drug Company 1988–1999	1988–1995	Early Management	‣ *Managed teams using continuous learning techniques in several diverse operating divisions.* ‣ Provided *financial leadership* on the multifunctional strategic team for the division's major product line. The team projects achieved annual cost reduction savings exceeding $3 million. ‣ Developed the strategic project model that was adopted by all commercial teams in the $1.5 billion Hospital Care Division that *streamlined investment decision making.* ‣ Researched, analyzed, and created financial pricing and P&L proposals to ensure risks were identified and mitigated for all the major hospital buying group contracts. ‣ Developed and *produced highly analytical* commercial sales and profit forecasts for the $100 million electronic drug delivery product line.

response will cause an interviewer to pause in any consideration of your assets. Here is an example:

Tough Q: "Tell me about your most significant failure on a job."

Wrong Answer: "I can't remember anything I have ever failed at."

This common answer is a big loser. People who say they have never failed can be divided into two categories: those who have never tried anything challenging enough that failure was a possibility, and those who do not have good self-awareness. Companies usually do not want anything to do with people in either category. Fortunately, you do not have to memorize the answers to tough questions because there is no single, best answer. Knowing how to approach them is a far superior technique.

As much as possible, for answers to these difficult questions, keep your answers simple, direct, and positive—make them affirmations of your fit with or interest in the position. In the example above, acknowledge the failures or difficulties that you have since corrected. For example, "Early in my career, I needed better project-management skills. These developed as I took project-management courses and gained more practical experience. . . ."

There are variations on this line of questioning. For example:

‣ Tell me about a time when you failed to deliver.

‣ What is your greatest weakness?

‣ What do you need to improve the most?

In each case, the interviewer wants to know what action you took to improve your skills and whether there are any lingering issues. You answer all questions about failures and shortcomings as examples of ways you became better over time. Avoid any suggestion that a weakness or shortcoming still exists to the *same extent* it did when first brought to your attention. Plus, this is an excellent time to return to your alignment sheet and mention a specific example of something you accomplished, putting it in the context of the value the company is seeking in filling the position.

For example, Michelle Street's résumé was, in part, written in response to the "key word" requirements that the successful candidate needs experience in training a staff. Here's her response to the question, "What is your greatest weakness?":

"Early in my career I was not as strong a leader as I needed to be. This showed up as impatience with staff any time we were under pressure to perform. Later, when I received the award for management excellence, it was obviously a team award. I led the team, but they did the work. I'm not sure we could have accomplished that earlier in my career."

From time to time, an interviewer will persist and ask for something you need to get better at right now. You should pick something that you worked on previously—that is, treat all "weaknesses" as opportunities for continuous improvement. For example, Michelle might respond, "Leadership skills require constant work."

QUESTIONS OF TIME GAPS Suppose the interviewer wants to know if there is a problem with you—perhaps how you work with people, if you have specific job-related skills, and so on. Because you've been out of work for a considerable time, the interviewer may suspect an underlying difficulty. The question may be indirect, but the objective is to find out why you were unemployed for a while.

What is considered a "long" time out of work varies, both with the economy and with individual situations. Recent college graduates can travel for up to a year without raising eyebrows. For more experienced workers, going more than a year between jobs qualifies as a "long" period.

No matter how long you have been out of work, you don't need to apologize or dwell on the subject. If you suspect your unemployment will last longer than six or seven months (a reasonable time to look for work), stay busy doing job-related tasks or volunteer work. All of us want our next jobs to be the right one, so some amount of continued unemployment can be explained as a search for the right job. But you must show that you have stayed busy in areas related to the job. For instance:

Q. "I noticed you have been out of work for fifteen months. Why has it taken so long to find another job?"

A. "Some of the time is the result of looking for the right opportunity with a company like yours. I have also used this time to give back to my church [or whatever institution] as an active volunteer."

Your answer will be stronger if your out-of-work activities have relevance to the skills required in the job. Again, look to your alignment sheet for guidance.

QUESTIONS ABOUT LEAVING YOUR LAST JOB People either leave a job voluntarily or are terminated. If you were terminated, you must work out with your previous employer how the termination will be characterized. Terminations can easily be positioned as voluntary leaves or job eliminations from restructurings. There is no disgrace in either situation. How you position that and what you say about it in the interview, however, are important.

The interviewer wants to know if you were fired from your last position and whether there is an underlying problem with you.

Q. "Did you leave your last job voluntarily?"

A. "I had a choice to make about whether I wanted to continue in a job with very little career upside. Since I needed to search for better opportunities full-time, I chose to look for a new position. If not, I would not have found this opportunity."

Of course, you must be ready to comment on the ways in which your opportunities at your old job were limited without bad-mouthing your previous employer.

QUESTIONS ABOUT CONFLICTS WITH FELLOW EMPLOYEES Questions about your working relationships in previous jobs are designed to uncover your familiarity with and use of conflict-management skills. The best skill to have in this area is the ability to bring people together to discuss the issues, assign roles, and move forward toward getting the job done. Even if you are not in a managerial position, potential employers will want to know what you did to help reduce the level and intensity of conflict.

The move toward flatter organizational structures requires greater skills to influence others and manage without authority. The interviewer wants to know how you behave in those environments. For example:

Q. "Tell me about a situation at work in which there was conflict among employees and how you handled it."

A. "One of our high-performing teams started bickering among themselves. Once I confirmed that others felt this way as well, I sponsored an off-site meeting facilitated by an outsider. It turned out that there was a lot of confusion about roles and responsibilities. Once these issues were clarified, the bickering stopped and productivity improved."

The suggestions here are not intended to cover every possible question type. There are many more questions you could be asked, and you can't, and shouldn't, try to prepare for all of them. Be willing to occasionally be surprised and have to think on your feet. An uncluttered mind is far more important than having practiced the answers to all the questions anyone would ever think to ask.

QUESTIONS OF SALARY Questions about salary can be particularly vexing in an interview because a wrong answer can eliminate you from competition, as well as compromise your bargaining position. If your previous salary was higher than what the company wants to pay, it may pick someone for whom its position would be a nice step up in compensation.

Many companies avoid hiring white-collar workers at lower pay levels than they had previously because of the concern that they will continue to search and use the current job as a temporary position until they find something better. On the other hand, if your previous salary was substantially below the position in question, a company may try to hire on the cheap.

If at all possible, deflect questions about salary and indicate that you would consider any offer the company thinks reasonable. If you are in a position where you can turn down job opportunities and wait until the right one comes along, you can afford to be more open about your salary requirements.

Some companies refuse to play the salary game and insist that you provide previous salary history or they will terminate your candidacy. If so, provide the information and proceed with the interview.

Questions for You to Ask

Always have a few questions ready to ask in return. Most interviewers will signal the end of the interview by asking, "Do you have any questions?" This does not mean you should wait until the end to ask your questions, however. If a question arises in the normal course of the interview, go ahead and ask it. However, hold a few back for the end.

This is not the time to show off your knowledge of recent company events in the news or to cover an arcane aspect of the industry. Follow the axiom to keep it simple. End-of-interview questions serve three purposes: to give you an opportunity to talk about aspects of the job for which you are a good fit but may not have been covered, to clear up any confusion, and to set the stage for follow-up steps. Though called "questions for the interviewer," the end of the interview is really a time for you to make affirmative statements about your candidacy and obtain the information you need for effective follow-up.

QUESTIONS THAT EMPHASIZE GOOD FIT Perhaps you are satisfied with how well the interviewer understands your fit with the job. If so, no questions in this area are required. The best way to determine that is to consult your alignment sheet. At this point, it is okay to actually pull the sheet out and glance over it to see if anything has been missed. You do not want to rustle through papers looking for the sheet. It should be right at your fingertips. For example:

Q. "I have covered what I need. Do you have any questions for me?"

A. "Let me check my notes." [Retrieve your alignment sheet and take a few seconds to review.] "I noticed in the position description that you wanted someone with experience in . . . . That's one of my strengths, and I want to make sure I have shared those details with you." [Unless interrupted, provide a brief description of what you accomplished.]

Or, the response might be:

A. "Let me check my notes. Earlier you asked me about . . . . I would like to add to that answer."

The second response gives you the opportunity to revisit an answer you want to improve on.

You might also ask questions as a way to clear things up. In a sense this is the same as the second response above. The interviewer's body language may have shown disagreement or confusion about an answer you gave. Now is your opportunity to clarify any misunderstanding. However, do not accuse the interviewer of misunderstanding or disagreeing, even if you feel he or she is at fault. Take responsibility for it by saying, "Perhaps what I said wasn't as clearly stated as it needed to be."

QUESTIONS ABOUT THE NEXT STEP You structure the end of the interview in a way that allows you to take positive action in the event you do not hear back in a timely manner. Hiring decisions are seldom made in the time frame initially laid out by the company. Candidates are often left twisting in the wind—or at least it feels that way. For you, the decision is monumentally important, whereas a company will likely have competing priorities. End the interview in a way that gives you permission to contact the company without appearing to be either overanxious or overbearing. For example:

> **Q.** "I have covered what I need. Do you have any questions for me?"

> **A.** "Let me check my notes [if appropriate]. When do you expect to make a decision?" [Wait for an answer.] "I will follow up in a couple of weeks just to check in."

Or,

> **A.** "My understanding is that you plan to make a decision by the middle of next month. Meanwhile, feel free to contact me if you have additional questions or something comes up. I will follow up as well."

❯   ❯   ❯

You have covered the basics of interviewing in a way that will help you prepare and relax so as to do your very best. The memorization requirements have been kept to a minimum. Nobody will ever know all of the answers to every possible question that can be asked. But if you know what is valued in the position, you can prepare for that moment when you can provide an answer that tells them what they really want to know.

• • • • • • • • • *Things to Remember* • • • • • • • • •

▶ *Because interviewing is more art than science, assessment tests are sometimes used to verify impressions gotten from interviews. Answer any assessment questions honestly and do not give the answers you think prospective employers want to hear. A good fit is as important for you as it is for them.*

▶ *To do your best, just relax. One of the best ways to relax is to be well prepared. Even well-prepared interviewees will still encounter questions and situations they did not anticipate.*

▶ *Preparation is required in three categories: protocols (etiquette), structure (kinds of interviews), and content (types of interview questions).*

▶ *Some questions are merely icebreakers while others have little evaluative meaning. Take all of them seriously.*

▶ *The answers to all interview questions are the same in that they all are opportunities to talk about things of value to the interviewer.*

▶ *Develop an alignment sheet using the key words from the position description and your résumé. Interviewers often use résumés to structure the interview, so organize those aspects of your résumé that refer directly back to what the interviewers are interested in. That linkage is the best expression of your fit with the position.*

▶ *Memorization comes into play when answering tough questions. A wrong answer can sink your candidacy. These include questions about weaknesses, long periods of unemployment, reasons for leaving other jobs, conflict management, and salary.*

RULE #5

You Get What You Negotiate, Not What You Deserve

CONGRATULATIONS! You have put value creation to work in your résumé, networking, and interviews. The end result is a job offer. The hunt is over. Now seems like a good time to relax. You tell yourself that you will take a few weeks off so you are rested and ready to hit the ground running.

Hold on! Did you get everything you set out to achieve when this process first started? Does your offer of employment have all of the conditions you want? Are the responsibilities of your next job as clear as they should be so you and your new employer will be happy together? These are only a few of the questions you need to consider before your new deal is final and you can relax.

During the time when changing jobs (and careers) was the exception rather than the rule, negotiation of the conditions of employment was not a skill worth perfecting. People expected to be at the same job for a long time, perhaps even until they retired. But times have changed. Today, negotiation skills are an absolute necessity for successful career management. The truth is that you are in your strongest bargaining position during the time between when a job is offered and when you accept it. The company has examined your credentials, invited you in for interviews, and decided to make an offer it hopes you will accept. You have more leverage now than at any other time. Take advantage of your strong position.

Taking advantage doesn't mean that you should make outrageous demands. It means that before accepting, you should review the situation and make sure you have what you wanted. Unless you take the time now to do some serious thinking, you run the risk of overlooking important considerations. Once you start a new job, it may be too late to do anything about them.

Here is a telling example. Joanne was so relieved to have finally landed a job that she accepted an offer of employment immediately, and she agreed to a start date without further discussion or review. "I have been out of work seven months," she thought. "I am happy and relieved just to have a job. Besides, people here seem flexible. If anything comes up, I'm sure we can work it out."

Joanne's feelings of goodwill were typical of the postoffer honeymoon, during which everyone is on his or her best behavior. Only later did Joanne discover that her new company counted tenure differently for vacation days. Her annual vacation time from the three weeks she had earned with her previous company was reduced to one week. Even worse, giving up two weeks of vacation may have been unnecessary. Later, she met fellow employees who had negotiated additional vacation days at their time of hire. This was doubly galling because the rate of vacation accrual was slower, and she would have to wait an additional five years just to get to two weeks. Six months into her job, her request for additional vacation time was turned down.

Perhaps you will review the offer you received, find out you are completely satisfied, and enter your new situation looking forward to work. But there is also a good chance you will discover opportunities to improve the conditions of your employment. You don't know what opportunities exist unless you learn how to look for them. The people who do that get what they negotiate, and not what they deserve.[1]

When you are offered a job, it is perfectly acceptable to say, "I really appreciate that we are at this point. I would like to take a little time to review the offer. Let me sleep on it and I will get back to you. What date works best?" Reputable companies understand the need for a little time between when an offer is made and when the candidate accepts. It is standard operating procedure. Be extra cautious if you are told, "Accept the offer now, or the deal is off."

Be Prepared to Negotiate

In labor negotiations, the parties don't wait until the contract expires to begin preparation for the next one. Likewise, the minute you know you might have to look for another job, you should give thought to what you want in a new position. This should be done well before a job offer is in hand.

At the very beginning of your job search you can effectively prepare for the negotiation phase by drawing up a list of things you want in a new position. Expect the list to change as you move through the job-search process. Date the list (and subsequent editions) to keep track of how it evolves. Once you complete an initial draft, put it away for review later after the completion of each major step in the job search. The items listed below are typical of the lists we have seen over the years:

Desirable Characteristics in My New Job (Middle Management)

- No more than 30 percent travel

- Company car

- Company-paid relocation

- Bonus opportunity of at least 40 percent

- Job-search support for spouse

- "Business casual" dress code

- Tuition reimbursement

- Adoption-support programs

▸ Company-paid health-club membership

▸ Day care on-site

▸ Work-life balance policy

▸ Preference for internal promotions

The list for more entry-level positions might be less specific, but the process is the same.

Desirable Characteristics in My New Job (Entry Level)

▸ Team-oriented supportive culture

▸ History of internal development and promotion

▸ Bonus opportunity

▸ Two weeks' vacation

▸ Financial stability

▸ No outsourcing

▸ Company-paid relocation

▸ Good reputation for hiring strong performers

▸ Performance-based culture

▸ Belief in work-life balance

▸ Challenging environment

▸ Pay for performance

▸ Health-care benefits

▸ "Business casual" work environment

Be sure the list represents your values and the things you feel you need in a new job. You must make distinctions, though, because not all of what you want will be available at the company, and it probably won't concede on every single item. Now, go back through the list and divide it into three categories: (1) What you absolutely must have, (2) What you would like to have, and (3) What you would like to have but can do without.

Try to put an equal number of items into each category. This is called a "flat" arrangement because it forces you to make hard choices early in the process, rather than loading everything into a couple of categories. As you come to understand the realities of your particular job market, these choices will likely move back and forth between the categories, giving you practice at making the compromises we all make as each job opportunity arises. For example, the unwillingness to relocate is usually one of the items that moves back and forth. For most, it is an unattractive alternative until you come face-to-face with relocating to another city or you will continue to be unemployed. Continual reevaluation of the list will also help you keep what's important to you in the forefront of your mind as you start your negotiations.

An example of how a middle-management list might be divided is shown in Figure 5.1. Use the same process for more entry-level positions.

FIGURE 5.1 *Job preferences.*

MUST-HAVES	LIKE TO HAVE	CAN DO WITHOUT
Vacation (3 weeks)	Job Search for Spouse	Business Casual Dress
Company-Paid Relocation	Company Car	Adoption Support
30% or Less Travel	Day Care On-Site	Work-Life Balance Policy
Bonus 40%+	Tuition Reimbursement	Internal Promotions

Know When to Negotiate

Preparation is helpful, but timing is crucial. If you communicate your preconditions to a company before you even land the job, you are violating the rule about delivering value first and foremost. The company will judge you against other job candidates, and those candidates may not stipulate any conditions. They will conduct their negotiations at the right time—after they are offered the job.

Jennifer learned this lesson the hard way. As for many professionals today, her life was filled with overlapping and sometimes conflicting roles—mother of two small children, married to a career-oriented professional, and needing two incomes to maintain their standard of living. Her ideal job would include the opportunity to work from home at least once or twice a week, as well as more flexible hours on days when she has to be in the office. Consequently, she specifically looked for companies that recognized the importance of work-life balance.

Jennifer decided to mention these preferences as often as appeared reasonable early in the interviewing process. She did not want to get all the way to the end and have the conditions be an insurmountable stumbling block. Unfortunately, she also gave the impression of less interest in what it would take to be an outstanding employee and more interest in what was in it for her. Even though the company had adopted a work-life balance as one of its core values, the job offer went to another candidate with similar requirements who had emphasized those needs less frequently during the interviews.

Jennifer understood her situation perfectly well. The problem was that she tried to negotiate the conditions of her employment too early. She allowed her work-life balance concerns to become too large a part of the decision-making calculus. That is, she got it backward. Companies hire people because of the perceived value they create, not because of the needs individual candidates have. While many companies are willing to accommodate those needs, the key factor in hiring is always value creation. Jennifer's forcing of the issue made her commitment to value creation look questionable, as well as unprofessional.

Generally speaking, no matter how important an issue is to you, you should raise it in earnest when you are in your strongest bargaining position—after an offer has been extended but before you accept. Until then, keep the conversation general. For example, it would be okay to ask, "I understand your company has a particular commitment to work-life balance. Can you please help me understand your policy?" Take note of the answer you get, but don't push it. In the meantime, look for other ways to determine if a particular company is right for you. For example, to test the company's commitment to work-life balance, Jennifer could have sought out women employees with children and learned firsthand from them how flexible the company was about hours. Perhaps she also could have found the information on the company website, in magazine articles, and/or from former employees. You don't have to ask your future boss directly.

Negotiation Outcomes

Of the four possible outcomes to a negotiation, three should be avoided. The four are:

1. Stalemate

2. I win/you lose

3. You win/I lose

4. Win/win

Undesirable outcomes result most often when one or both parties misunderstand the bargaining stage of the job-negotiation process. Keep in mind that you are at the most desirable point in your job search. You want a job, have found an employer that offered one, and have a most favorable environment for negotiation. Win/win is the most desirable outcome.

In the heat that sometimes accompanies negotiation, both parties can forget that most of what they are trying to accomplish has been completed. Often the last step to the end goal is a short one. Poorly understood negotiations run the risk of doing damage to a future relationship and may reach the point of ruining the deal altogether.

STALEMATE

A stalemate occurs when one party to a negotiation wants something the other party is unwilling to give. This happened to Bart when he insisted that his new salary be at least a 10 percent increase over what he had earned previously. He had always believed that each new job should be bigger and better than the previous one. To him, the most important measurement of career advancement was salary progression.

But the company's offer was a full 10 percent below what Bart had previously earned. Though the initial conversations about salary level were pleasant, neither side was willing to give an inch. Neither could get past a fixed point of view. The company wanted to pay only so much for the position, and Bart wanted a clear demonstration of career progression. They were at a stalemate.

Alternative forms of compensation during the first year of employment could have been considered as a way to make up the difference. These options include sign-on bonuses, extra vacation, or commitments to do salary reviews at six-month intervals to determine if an employee's contribution warrants additional consideration. A compensation package can have many components, so make sure you try different avenues to reach the same goal. A show of flexibility can induce the other side to be flexible as well.

I WIN/YOU LOSE AND YOU WIN/I LOSE

These two positions can be viewed similarly because they are mirror images of one another. Both parties see negotiation as a zero-sum game in which a gain for one side is a loss for the other. This happened to Steve when he listed his job priorities but did not sort them further. He negotiated for all the items as though losing any one of them was a gain for the company he was negotiating with. He forgot that, at this stage in his job search, he and the company agreed on many more things than they disagreed on. Now would have been a good time to revisit his list to see what trade-offs were possible.

So, pay special attention to the category of things that would be nice to have but you could do without. You may be able to trade some of those as "give-backs." Also, reassess those priorities that were once seen as nonnegotiable "must-haves." Given the specific conditions of the job offer, some of those items may now seem less important.

WIN/WIN

Mutually satisfying situations are created when you discover common ground on which both parties can agree and each side gets enough of what it needs to feel good about the outcome. Win/win outcomes provide the basis for the ongoing relationship that you will have if you take the job.

Not that every negotiation will result in a win/win, but with a little bit of skill and perseverance, compromise is possible most of the time. Here is where good listening skills definitely come into play. Since an immediate answer is not required, you don't have to formulate one before the offer has been fully presented. Listen carefully all the way to the end of the offer presentation. Offers of employment usually lead with the most positive features: "Tom, we are pleased to extend this offer to work for us at the salary we agreed to."

But the devil is always in the details, and eventually they will mention any downsides—and sometimes they fail to mention them at all. Either way, you need to pay attention. Regardless of any disappointment you feel at first about certain conditions, maintain the positive attitude that is part of any win/win negotiation. You may need the goodwill it generates later if the back-and-forth negotiation gets testy. You would need years of practice in negotiating the conditions of your employment to become an expert negotiator. Most likely, you do not want to change jobs and careers that often, but let's move to discussing some of the basics of skillful negotiation.

Seven Rules for Skillful Negotiation

You can become competent enough to get what you want as long as you understand some basic rules. These seven rules for skillful negotiation are designed to make you a proficient negotiator in your own cause. Three of the seven (3, 4, and 7) can be found in almost any good book on negotiation; the other four (1, 2, 5, and 6) are unique to this book.

1. NEVER TURN DOWN A JOB BEFORE IT IS OFFERED

You may wonder if anyone really does that. But it happens all the time, and that is why we mention it first. Remember, you get what you negotiate, and that can include a variety of added benefits. You can collect extra compensation, as we have seen, and even a better job title.

Donna didn't know that, and she paid the price. She had worked hard to climb the corporate ladder and was pleased when she finally was promoted from a director to vice president. Yet her excitement was short-lived owing to a restructuring in which management layers were thinned and her newly attained vice president's position was eliminated. The outplacement firm warned that the trend toward flattened organizational structures had gained momentum, and she would likely find fewer VP positions in the industry as a whole. She viewed taking another director-level position as a step backward. For that reason, she had a VP title on her list of "must-haves."

In the beginning stages of her search, Donna declined an opportunity to interview for a director of marketing position for the U.S. division of a multinational beverage company. The firm had only one VP-level marketing position, and that had just been filled. She felt the job was in a smaller division and at a lower level than she wanted.

A couple of months later, she agreed to be a reference for a former colleague who interviewed for the same director of marketing position Donna had turned down. When she was notified that her colleague was the successful candidate, Donna called to offer congratulations. To her shock, she learned that the position had been upgraded to the VP level, with a corresponding adjustment in salary.

"How did that happen?" Donna asked.

"It was part of the negotiation. The job had been identified as a future VP-level position, but they were willing to upgrade it now to get the right person."

Titles, salary levels, and many other aspects of a future job can be negotiated. But unless you get the offer, you'll never find out. If some aspect of a new job becomes a nonnegotiable that you cannot resolve, you can always turn the job down. But don't turn down an otherwise attractive opportunity until you have had the chance to negotiate.

Another reason people turn jobs down before they are offered is to protect their self-esteem. If they suspect their chances of getting an offer are not as good as they should be, they sometimes withdraw from the competition. A lot of excuses come into play: "It would have been a step backward." "I've done that job before." Needless to say, turning jobs down before they are offered limits your options.

2. USE THIRD-PARTY NEGOTIATORS WHEN POSSIBLE

Using an outside party to negotiate a better deal gives you a chance to raise sensitive issues safely. You can ask these touchy questions directly; however, the negotiation process may be more comfortable for both sides if you go through a third party.

For example, Ruth was a single parent with a special-needs child. From time to time she had to either leave work early or come in late when her caregiver required more flexible hours. She was reluctant to bring the issue up before the offer sheet was signed, and she approached the search firm about the best way to proceed. The search consultant knew the company well, recognized its willingness to deal with such issues, and advised Ruth to alert the references from her previous job to include positive comments about how she handled the situation—that her circumstances in no way ever affected the quality of her work and required special arrangements only two or three times a year. The search consultant presented the information to the company and likened the situation to that of another of the employees the company liked very much. Everyone was satisfied and the job offer went forward without a hitch.

If you thought the search firm was paid by and working for the company, you are correct. Is it smart, therefore, to let the search firm do your bidding? Yes, and it works almost every time. Here is why. Remember, you are at that special stage during negotiations when you have maximum leverage. That leverage extends to search firms as well. That is, everyone concerned thinks you are the best candidate for the position. The search firm has satisfied its basic obligation to the client and is now looking for its cut. The firm has extra incentive to negotiate any remaining items as quickly as possible. At this stage of the game there are plenty of incentives to achieve a win/win result.

Third parties, such as search firms, can probe sensitive topics like salary, job title, time off, and other factors without creating the appearance that your demands are unreasonable or that you are difficult to deal with. Some direct negotiations become so contentious that they poison the employer/employee relationship before it gets going. Rather than hitting the ground running, you spend your first few months on the job mending fences.

Generally, the lower the position in the organization, the less you need a third-party negotiator. For senior-level and upper-middle-management positions, an employment lawyer is highly recommended, however. For most situations, it is not a good idea to put your lawyer between you and a new employer unless it is the norm to do so. Negotiations with professional athletes, authors, entertainers, actors, and very senior-level people often involve third parties. The contracts can be complicated and require considerable expertise. Most lawyers, however, work better behind the scenes, pointing out areas for additional negotiation and where clarifications are needed.

Because the revolving employment door could start spinning at any time, many executives are advised at this time to also negotiate the conditions of their terminations, including severance pay, outplacement, stock-option exercise rights, and other matters. Some executives have even negotiated the continued use of the company plane and an expense account to carry them through to the next position.

3. GET IT IN WRITING

Most job-hunting books advise you to not resign from your old job until you have the new offer in hand. Even then, an offer may confirm intent, but it may not actually constitute a legal obligation for employment. Any changes in business conditions (mergers, acquisitions, divestitures, etc.) could cause a job offer to be rescinded.

The last word Derrick heard from the HR representative after his final interview was, "We are good to go with an offer of employment." He jumped the gun and resigned from his old company right away. That night, he was dismayed by the call from that same HR rep, who informed him, "Something came up and there will be a delay in getting that offer letter to you." Eventually, it worked out, but he had to go through a couple of uncomfortable days, having resigned from his former company without confirmation of a job offer from another.

Also, read your offer letter carefully. It probably contains all sorts of qualifiers about not intending to create an "implied" contract. Employment lawyers routinely advise companies to limit their offer letters to start date and salary. As a result, details about other conditions of employment may be intentionally omitted. Most companies are willing to go further, but the language they use will in all likelihood be approved by legal counsel.

Since many offer letters are carefully scripted to give the advantage to the company in the event a dispute arises, you should have your offer for more senior-level positions reviewed by counsel as well, especially if you have negotiated any exceptions to the company's general policy. Companies usually reserve the right to rescind offers if business conditions warrant, and from time to time that happens. An offer in writing confirms the company's commitment to all the details necessary to move forward.

In certain cases, negotiated conditions of employment are complicated, and a written offer letter gives you an opportunity to clarify any commitments before it is too late to do anything about them. Plus, you have additional time to review your list of "must-haves" and determine if the new job includes all of them. If not, you still have time to revisit the details of the offer and have them adjusted.

4. KNOW HOW YOU STACK UP AGAINST THE COMPETITION

If you are the only viable candidate for the position, your bargaining position is much stronger than if you are one of several possible candidates. Gaining access to that information may be difficult, however, and you should plan to conduct your negotiation without it. At critical times during your interviews you might be able to get a strong indication of what the company's situation is. For example, you are likely to have more bargaining power if the job for which you are interviewing is considered critical and has been vacant for a long time. Those extreme cases are easy to decipher. One way to dig out the information is to ask questions about how long the job has been open and how critical it is to running the organization. Obviously, such questions are less appropriate for lower-level positions.

5. UNDERPLAY YOUR HAND

Some people pride themselves on never leaving a dime on the negotiating table. That strategy is a mistake because it forces you to haggle over issues that are relatively unimportant. Your list of priorities is, in part, designed to help make distinctions among what you must have and what it'd be nice to have.

Ed was a haggler by nature, and he did not draw up a list of priorities beforehand. As a result he argued each item in his negotiation as if all were of equal importance. The hole he dug became deeper and deeper. The hiring manager started to wonder if the skills Ed brought to the company were worth the hassle. The company did not like what they saw when Ed did not get his way.

Lower-priority items provide a good way to make gracious negotiating concessions. They show that you are willing to see the other side of an issue and accept someone else's best thinking. You give up an item on your list to foster an image of being a reasonable employee. In this sense, you have underplayed your hand and did not get all you bargained for. But you also demonstrated a willingness to compromise for a larger good.

6. UNDERPROMISE AND OVERDELIVER

During negotiations, you must make a major mind shift in how you approach the process. Until now, you have emphasized all the wonderful things you have accomplished and the match of these accomplishments to the requirements of the job.

Once a job offer is in hand, most candidates continue to charge ahead, perhaps promising more than they can deliver in the time frame others ask. That's a mistake—a major mistake. It is now time to change gears.

Expectations help shape how your performance on the job will be perceived. An example from the world of customer service demonstrates this point. At a bank in Westchester County, New York, wait times at bank branches was an important customer-service issue. Customer complaints grew in proportion to the wait times. A debate ensued as to the best way to improve customer service. As an experiment, the wait time in one branch was reduced from nine to six minutes during peak hours of branch usage by adding additional staff—an expensive solution. In another branch (the one it took the staff from), wait times went from nine to twelve minutes. But to alert customers to the prospect of longer waits, an electronic display of "anticipated wait time until the next teller is available" was adjusted to a time that was always greater than the actual wait.

What was the result? Customer satisfaction in the branch with longer wait times rose dramatically. At the same time, it remained the same for the branch with lower wait times. Bank management concluded that the newly created expectations led to the "appearance" of better customer service and to greater customer satisfaction, even though the wait times were actually longer.

The same principle is at work when you start a new job. New employees have a tendency to make exaggerated promises about what they can do and how quickly they can do it. Yet research clearly proves that overpromising and underdelivering is a significant factor in determining poor performance and is a significant cause of new executive terminations.

It is better to set expectations you can exceed than ones you can't possibly meet. Once an offer is made, and as you are asked to make performance commitments, tone down your eagerness to demonstrate a "can-do" attitude and make measured promises about your performance. Then deliver ahead of schedule. A few times of exceeding expectations will help create a positive perception of how well you are doing.

7. NEVER END THE NEGOTIATING GAME

Well-run companies treat high-performing employees better than other employees. And high-performing employees are perceived as the ones who create value. An important part of any job is to continue to create value for your employer in the same way as you positioned your skills when you first applied. You should from time to time review the position description and the résumé you tweaked for it. The alignment between the two documents represents the value the company looked to create when it filled the position. Your new job is to create that value or its equivalent, over and over again.

There will always be circumstances beyond your control and jobs will continue to be eliminated regardless of how much value you create. But the unyielding focus on value creation lays the groundwork for your next job search. That focus can put you in the category of people who find new jobs rather easily and cause other people to wonder what you know that they don't.

▶   ▶   ▶

Your next job is always right around the corner. Sometimes that's because your current one has been eliminated and/or because you consciously choose to do something different. The skills and information you need to make that choice is the subject of the next chapter.

• • • • • • • • • *Things to Remember* • • • • • • • • •

▶ *The time between a job offer and your acceptance is special. You have maximum bargaining power and the ability to get what you negotiate, rather than necessarily what you deserve.*

▶ *Prepare for negotiation early by establishing a list of "must-haves," "would like to have," and "would like to have but am willing to do without." The list will act as a constant reminder of what's important.*

▶ *The best time to negotiate is once you have an offer, rather than during the interviewing process.*

▶ *The four negotiation outcomes are stalemate, I win/you lose, you win/I lose, and win/win. Win/win is the most desirable outcome because it gives both parties enough of what they need to establish a healthy post-negotiation relationship.*

▶ *You don't have to become an expert negotiator. If you follow seven rules of negotiation, you will secure the conditions of employment you want. These are:*

(1) never turn down a job before it is offered, (2) use third-party negotiators when possible, (3) get it in writing, (4) know how you stack up against the competition, (5) underplay your hand, (6) underpromise and overdeliver, and (7) never end the negotiating game.

NOTE

1. Chester L. Karrass, *In Business as in Life, You Don't Get What You Deserve, You Get What You Negotiate* (Stanford Street Press, 1996).

$\#6$
R U L E

Career Choice Is More Than Following Your Passion

A FEW SUMMERS ago one of our networking groups discussed how the members' career choices might have been different if they knew then what they know now. Some had changed careers before, while others were doing so for the first time. Everyone, however, felt dissatisfied about the process. They all wanted to know: What is the best way to go about making a career choice? What factors are important and in what order do you rank them? Even those who had approached the subject in a systematic way ended up feeling that what they had learned was too mechanical to be helpful. On the other hand, those who tried to find a job they were passionate about had just as much trouble. To them, a job was still a job.

Members were asked to submit a list of topics for discussion, and the lists were then circulated to determine the level of interest in each topic. Each meeting was devoted to a single topic, and an agenda was produced ahead of time so only those interested would attend. Career choice turned out to be a popular topic for the group members. Word of the session spread, and it has become a favorite subject for other networking groups as well.

Just why this topic is of so much interest is obvious. Many people don't know how to go about choosing a career, or they may be unhappy with the choice they made years ago, or perhaps the economy is forcing a change upon them. This chapter looks at the career decision: how it is commonly made, what's faulty about that decision, how to make a better decision, where to look for help, and how opportunity comes along when you least expect it.

Career Choice: Information Aplenty but Little Guidance

A wealth of anecdotal evidence supports the view that white-collar workers are interested in changing careers now more than at any other time in history. Dissatisfaction with original career choices, limited career prospects in particular fields, and other factors have influenced much of this thinking. With advances in technology and globalization, career change has become not only more possible but also more necessary. Not only jobs but also entire careers have disappeared and new ones have emerged to take their place. White-collar workers have had to adjust accordingly. They move from job to job and career to career as needed—a far cry from the days when we thought of a white-collar job as a lifetime commitment.

Every year, thousands of graduates are choosing careers for the first time. There is no shortage of written material or career consultants available to help. Indeed, once you start this process, you will discover a virtual mountain of information. The problem is that the advice is difficult to wade through and confusing, to boot. For example, the bible for career information is the government's *Occupational Outlook Handbook,* published by the Bureau of Labor Statistics (BLS). Its almost 1,000 pages contain everything anyone wants to know about occupations in America. And each state has its own equivalent resource for jobs inside its borders. Yet we defy any but the most expert in the field of career management to use these heavy tomes to determine a person's career direction.

Other, almost equally voluminous secondary sources help you use the data collected by the BLS. Two very good ones are Michael Farr's *Top 100 Careers for College*

Graduates and *College Majors Handbook: With Real Career Paths and Payoffs.* Yet most students will get lost reading any of these works on their own. And more experienced professionals wanting to change careers won't likely find them useful, either. Additional secondary resources that some have used effectively include *What Color Is Your Parachute?* (Richard Nelson Bolles), *Life's a Bitch and Then You Change Careers* (Andrea Kay), and *The Pathfinder* (Nicholas Lore).

Regardless of whether you are wanting to change your career or are a student making an initial choice of career, you should read everything you reasonably can, find a reputable career consultant if you have the money, and make a solid decision. For more experienced workers, one of the deterrents to career change is a reluctance to switch horses in midstream. After years of being identified as a professional in one area, it is difficult to give up the money and training so as to switch to an unrelated field, especially if that new field requires additional preparation.

But before you consider any of that, this chapter presents the advice gleaned from our networking groups. In particular, it helps you avoid being overwhelmed by too much information. Similarly, the idea of changing careers is a relatively recent development, and quality advice on the matter has barely kept pace. Much of what we sense about career change is grounded in a misunderstanding of work itself. In particular, the group concluded that the role passion plays in career choice is overrated, whereas the role of serendipity is underrated. To make a solid career choice, the group concluded, college students need to select fields of study that require skills they enjoy doing and are good at deploying, and for which there is—and will continue to be—wide demand.

Passion and Career Choice

Let's take a look at two examples of why passion and work may not be the same thing. Don and Stephanie left the suburban life of Connecticut and the substantial income from his investment banking practice, and they moved to Vermont. There, he ran a small, but successful opinion-research firm and she opened an interior-design business. Geoff, a member of our initial networking group, was in pharmaceutical sales in Southern California. After the last layoff, he and his wife, Ellen (an RN), picked up, moved back to rural Minnesota, and opened a general store.

Don and Stephanie are usually the first ones to admit that the move to Vermont had nothing to do with a passion for their new work there. Their decision had more to do with lifestyle preferences than anything else. The daily grind of commuting to New York City and long hours at work left them little time for much else. They belong to a new generation of workers who when asked if they want more free time or higher salary respond that time is far more important than money.

The same was true for Geoff and Ellen. Their passion was for a simpler lifestyle than what they had in California. All through high school and college, Geoff was intensely interested in studying chemistry. To him, pharmaceuticals seemed like a natural career choice. But once employed, he learned that a career in this field was less interesting than what he enjoyed studying in college.

The idea that passion should guide our career choices is appealing. All of us would like to live in a world in which what we do for a living is a continual source of inspiration and satisfaction. But that does not happen very often. Most people know what they are passionate about—or at least what they most enjoy doing. Identifying our passions is not the problem. The difficulty is linking those passions to available work. The interaction between what we do for a living and what makes us happy has many sides. And the advice to follow your passion to find work often distorts as much as it clarifies.

Take, for example, the commencement exercises on college campuses across the nation each year. For decades, commencement speakers have told newly minted graduates to "follow their passion." We now have several generations of graduates who believe they should be passionate about what they do for a living. If not, they will lead less fulfilling lives. The secret here is that, over time, any job has elements of drudgery; passion cannot be sustained uninterrupted. At those times, you may wonder why your job is supposed to represent your life's passion.

PASSION AS THE BASIS FOR CAREER CHOICE

A belief in following your passion has merit. For example, children and adults do better at tasks they like than those they dislike. Plus, empirical evidence shows that our passion for some activity or subject helps us stay the course when the going gets tough. So what's the problem? It's that people leap to conclusions and apply too broad a stroke to what they see as the benefits of passion.

Career counselors are sometimes guilty of this, too. Those in the outplacement industry, in particular, tend to genuflect before the idea that white-collar professionals should be in tune with what they "really want." If you can find work you are passionate about, the argument goes, you will be happier, more productive, and more successful. So, people embark on a journey looking for their life's passion as if it were the only key to career success. Sometimes that search works out and sometimes it doesn't—especially now.

Much of the advice about following one's passions is a matter of oversimplification. This tendency toward generalization is nothing new in the literature of career management. In the early 1970s, social scientists studied business leaders to find out how they became leaders. Many attributed much of their success to the presence of mentors. Researchers consequently recommended that companies identify the people they want to succeed and assign them mentors, in an effort to move them along more quickly. Only later did it become clear that company-imposed mentoring relationships do not work nearly as well as those that occur naturally. And in some cases, the effects of mentoring were reversed; that is, when orchestrated by the company, the mentoring did more harm than good. That's because mentees began to ignore peer relationships, which were later also identified as important contributing factors to success within organizations. Nonetheless, the popularity of mentoring persisted. Today, there is a National Mentoring Association, as well as a National Mentoring Month. Few doubt that mentoring can be an effective way to influence careers, but it, like following your passion, has limitations.

AN OVERRATED DETERMINER

Those who look at career success solely through the prism of their passion can be in for a long and frustrating experience. Rather than having unbridled enthusiasm, most white-collar professionals we have spoken with feel ambivalent about their work. They—and countless others like them—want to like what they do for a living and feel a sense of obligation to their employers to do a good job, but they also relish their leisure time and always seem to want more of it.

Bernie had an undergraduate degree in engineering and an MBA from a well-respected university. Yet his job was outsourced twice—once to a domestically based competitor and another time to a venture-capitalist upstart in China. Unsure of what else to do, he planned to return to school to study photography—his "real passion."

He eventually realized there were plenty of good reasons to return to school, and under the right circumstances, photography could be one of them. But the reeducation decision needed more consideration than simply how it aligned with his passion. He needed a more complete perspective on his future job prospects.

Attitudes Toward Work

The following three themes emerged from our group discussions about what we think about work. For many, work is a *moral obligation.* Hardworking people are good people, with strong ethics. The best people are those for whom work is pleasure and pleasure is work. Great pleasure in life comes from the quality of work we do. This is what people mean when they speak of the "work ethic" in the United States.

Work is also viewed as a *contractual agreement,* in which both sides sacrifice to contribute to a common goal. This view gained favor with the rise of white-collar professionals. Workers were asked to show their loyalty to the company and make personal sacrifices in exchange for secure employment, the possibility of training and promotions, and a pension in retirement. These were often referred to as the "golden handcuffs" because they served to keep workers on the job and in line with company policy. Though those contractual agreements began to disappear as companies shifted work elsewhere, the desire for them still exists. Even today, most unemployed white-collar workers begin their job search by looking for organizations that are "loyal to their employees." They prefer companies that are reluctant to outsource or downsize when there are downturns in the business environment.

In contrast, today there is widespread understanding that jobs, and careers, are based on little more than a *self-interested* contractual exchange of "you scratch my back and I'll scratch yours." But most of us still want jobs and careers that are more than that. We want to like what we do, feel good about it, and fulfill obligations to something more than ourselves. That is why making a good career choice involves more than having a passion for your work.

Resources for Making Solid Career Choices

Our networking groups readily acknowledged that people need a range of information to make solid career choices. In varying combinations, that range includes an understanding of one's interests, values, personality, and aptitude, as well as how to prepare for work and what the future demands will be for particular kinds of work. All of these topics are covered in career guides. However, the assessments contained therein vary widely in their usefulness.

Let's start at the bottom of the job scale, at entry-level jobs. Because of the large volume of information available, students should use selective resources available from high schools and colleges and universities, rather than wade through all of them on their own. Trained career counselors on campus can provide access to various skills assessments at no cost, along with assistance in interpreting the scores to determine your career direction.

Adults seeking information on career change should do much the same. If you are a college graduate, check with the placement center where you went to school to see if they have assessment services for alumni. Seek professional guidance, as well, because our most consistent source of misinformation about our skills, talents, and temperament is ourselves. You've heard the expression, "A lawyer who represents himself has a fool for a client." We wouldn't go quite that far in describing self-evaluation abilities, but most people are not impartial judges of their own abilities. So, if you can afford a professional service, there are many dedicated professionals willing to help. Do an Internet search on career coaches. Be aware that there are no uniform standards for performance in the field, so ask for references and proof of certification that may exist.

Not everyone, however, has the resources for, or access to, professional career counseling. Self-assessment is still a reasonable alternative, and you can find an abundance of tools to help you, many free of charge. Because there are hundreds of options, you will save time by using reliable resources that have already organized and prioritized the information for you. These are called assessment industry synthesizers, and the information they provide generally goes beyond self-assessment tools and includes explanations on how to use the results. Some are listed below.

GENERAL GOVERNMENT RESOURCES

O*NET is the primary online source for occupational information and it is sponsored by the U.S. Department of Labor. In 2000, it produced a fifty-five-page PDF document entitled "Tests and Other Assessments: Helping You Make Better Career Decisions," available at www.onetcenter.org/dl_files/testAsse.pdf. More recent editions are provided as online updates.

The O*NET document is a useful synopsis of various information sources on assessments, including how counselors and employers use them and where to go for testing. The assessments are defined as follows:

Achievement tests measure how well you know a subject.

Skills tests measure how you can perform for a particular job.

Interest inventories help you identify your interests, especially those related to work. These tests have no right or wrong answers.

Work values tests allow you to pinpoint what you value in jobs (such as achievement, autonomy, support, and conditions of work).

Personality assessments help identify your personal style in dealing with tasks, data, and other people. Your personality may be best suited for certain kinds of work.

The O*NET resource helps cut through the professional jargon of personal assessments so you have a good idea of what is being measured. You can then use other guides to find the type of work you might find rewarding.

OTHER MAJOR RESOURCES

Other (mostly nongovernmental) integrators include:

▸ *The Riley Guide* (Self Assessment Resources) is a directory of employment and career-information services available on the Internet (www.rileyguide.com/teen .html). Its author/owner, Margaret Dikel (formerly Margaret Riley), is a librarian specializing in online architecture design and search. *The Riley Guide* is among the oldest and best of its kind and can be recommended without reservation. The guide contains straightforward, easy-to-understand definitions of "personality" and "type" that help you understand how you take in information, how you prefer to make decisions, what energizes you, and whether you prefer to keep your objectives open-ended or move toward conclusion. This information, in conjunction with support provided by the *Occupational Outlook Handbook* and the *College Majors Handbook,* mentioned earlier, can be useful in understanding the occupations for which you may be a good fit.

In *The Riley Guide* you will also find that brief descriptions and access information are provided for the different categories of assessments, some of which are listed below:

Personality Type: Myers-Briggs; Keirsey Temperament Sorter; iMapMyLife.com

Interest Inventories: What Color Is Your Parachute?; Career Key; Campbell Interest and Skill Survey (via USNews.com); Campbell Interest and Skill Survey (via NCS Pearson); Career Test from Career Planners.com; Focus Career and Educational Planning; MAPP (Motivational Assessment of Personal Potential); Self-Directed Search

Skill Surveys: Skills Center; What's Your Skillset; Career Assessment Exercises

▶ *About.com* has a good section on career tests (many online and free) that you can use to determine "what you want to do when you grow up." It is suggested that you take a couple of tests from its list of suggested resources, and then move to a more in-depth assessment that, when a fee is involved, may well be worth the investment. They suggest and briefly describe the Myers-Briggs Type Indicator (MBTI), Career Key, Discover Your Perfect Career Quiz, Keirsey Temperament Sorter, Princeton Review Quiz, Strong Interest Inventory, and other personality tests from their directory of online general and personality tests.

As with other sources mentioned here, the information from About.com is reliable and relatively complete with regard to self-assessment instruments, especially those that may involve more interpretive support.

▶ *QuintessentialCareers.com* has an "Online Career Assessment Tools Review for Job Seekers and Career Seekers" section. This guide summarizes thirty career-assessment instruments; shares cost information, which varies from free to as much as $80; describes what each assessment measures; reports on its ease of use; and evaluates how useful each assessment is, based on the experience of Quintessential staff, clients, and students. The highest-rated assessments include Campbell Skill and Interest Inventory ($18), Career Liftoff Interest Inventory ($19.95), Career Maze ($19.95); Career Values Scale from testingroom.com ($14.95), Jackson Vocational Interest Survey ($19.95), and the Keirsey Temperament Sorter (free). Some instruments provide two levels of feedback—those you get for free and more detailed assessments that cost money. Quintessential lets you know if it perceives different levels of usefulness between the two.

▸ The "Find Assessment" section at www.careeronestop.org is also operated by the U.S. Department of Labor, and readers are encouraged to use the following assessments:

Skills Profiler. Creates a list of your existing skills.

O*NET's *Ability Profiler.* Identifies your strengths and areas where more training may be required.

O*NET's *Interests Profiler.* Helps you understand the type of work you would find interesting.

O*NET's *Work Importance Locator.* Identifies features about jobs that are important to you.

O*NET's *Employability Checkup.* Helps you determine if you are ready for the work environment.

The O*NET resources are specifically designed to be used by workers across a broad spectrum. They do not assume you have a college degree or are working toward one. They will tell you what kind of work most closely fits your profile and what additional training may be required.

The Role of Serendipity in Career Choice

If you are not from New Orleans, you've probably never heard of the legendary Sidney Torres. He is a garbageman. More accurately, perhaps, he owns STD Waste and Debris Services and has the contract to pick up the garbage in the French Quarter. You can see him almost anytime, day or night, riding (occasionally driving) one of several trucks that often operate on-call to pick up unsightly waste and scrub the streets to rid the Quarter of unpleasant odors. Mr. Torres is a Connecticut prep school graduate, an LSU dropout, and a former personal assistant to rock star Lenny Kravitz. But he is best known for his garbage-collection activities. It is not unusual for a passerby to shout out his name or for small crowds of people to stand and applaud as he and his crew clean the streets.

For all the talk of passion, and all the self-assessment tests you can take, there's one part of career planning that cannot be overlooked: serendipity. People "fall into" jobs that they never expected, and they find that they derive true satisfaction from their unexpected employment. A chance referral from a friend inside a company can lead to a new career. Or, if you are more independently minded, you strike out on your own in a direction that you could not have planned back in college—or even six months ago.

You would not have predicted that Sidney Torres would end up in garbage collection, based on his previous experiences. Yet he has considerable interest, aptitude, and passion for this work. Immediately before the waste-services business, he was a real estate developer—a business initially financed by a $100,000 loan co-signed by his grandmother. Now, still in his early thirties, he owns several companies, including this multimillion-dollar waste-services business, he was named a 2007 "Hero" by the New Orleans Convention Bureau, and he has received several other awards as well—all because of his knack for garbage collection.

Torres did not arrive at his position through any of the career instruments previously discussed, however, or by following his passion. The route he took to his present career is the result of serendipity. As our careers unfold, unplanned events and circumstances enter into the mix and present as many opportunities as they do challenges. The important question is, how will we respond?

The unplanned event in Torres's career was Hurricane Katrina. Rather than leave the city, as residents had been advised to do, Torres stayed and leased his real estate properties to incoming emergency personnel who needed living quarters and other services. Torres quickly developed a reputation for being able to supply everything from drinking water to emergency medical services.

As the aftereffects of Katrina became obvious, Torres was asked by city officials to help in a number of ways, such as finding a replacement for the disposal company, which had abandoned its contract. Unable to find a suitable alternative, Torres located a couple of trucks and did the job himself. Authorities thought that the local economy would recover more quickly if tourists could be convinced that the French Quarter was safe and clean. But STD Waste Services did more than pick up the garbage. It scrubbed the streets clean practically on demand. And the French Quarter opened for business much sooner than anyone had anticipated. Sidney Torres became a local hero and business success.

Just as much as passion is overrated in terms of career choice, so serendipity is underrated. Never allow the process of career choice blind you to unanticipated opportunities. Some professionals evolve on a straight line from what they studied in college to what they do for a career. In our experience, many more cannot trace their career path so easily, however. And most acknowledge the role of an accidental dimension that led to the direction their career eventually took.

You never know when lightning will strike. Some famous people started late, before they made the career choice in which they excelled. Colonel Sanders opened his first Kentucky Fried Chicken restaurant when he was sixty-five. Grandma Moses started painting when she was in her seventies. And Laura Ingalls Wilder didn't complete her most famous book, *Little House on the Prairie,* until well into her sixties.

Other people start one career and finish in another one altogether. Julia Child was a spy for the U.S. government before she became a cookbook author; Martha Stewart was a stockbroker before she became a lifestyle trendsetter; James Joyce was a professional singer before he became an author. How they got from one place to another always had a certain element of serendipity, and the same is true for many more ordinary people as well.

You cannot prepare for serendipity, of course, but you will be better positioned to take advantage of it if you embrace the following:

1. Learn to create value in whatever you do. With technology and globalization, the demand for value is at an all-time high. During these times, your brand (reputation) becomes more, not less, important.

2. The value you create is not about you, but what others want from you and your ability to provide it. It works in finding employment and changing careers.

3. The market for the value you create may not be hidden so much as it is splintered. Make sure the value you create is on full display when opportunity knocks.

▶   ▶   ▶

There is a subset of professionals who exit and reenter the job market in predictable ways and for predictable reasons. Women often fit into this category. As such, they are in a unique position to take special advantage of the 7 Rules. That is the topic of the next chapter.

• • • • • • • • • • *Things to Remember* • • • • • • • • • •

▶ *The role that passion plays in career choice is overrated.*

▶ *For career advice, use professional career counselors. If you want to find a career choice on your own, use one of the several resource integrators to guide you.*

▶ *Don't become mechanical in your approach. Serendipity can play a major role in whatever career you eventually choose.*

▶ *To take advantage of opportunities, remember to continue to create value for your employer; recognize that value creation is not about you, but what others want from you; and when the opportunity presents itself, make sure the value you create is on full display.*

#7

R U L E

The Best Way to Reenter the Job Market Is to Never Leave It

LET'S FACE IT: in the job market, women are different. This is not an admission of failure in the battle for equal pay and a more just society. Yet the truth is that the road to career success for professional women remains more complicated and more difficult than it is for men. This observation has two important consequences. First, changes in the rules for finding white-collar employment play out differently for women. Second, failure to take these differences into consideration can have disastrous consequences.

The difference in job situations for men and women was driven home dramatically by Allison O'Kelly, founder and CEO of Mom Corps, a staffing company designed to help professional women reenter the workforce and establish work-life alignment. "I knew there had to be a better way," she confessed, "when as a seventeen-year-old my father died suddenly and my mother had to reinvent the career she put off to raise a family."[1] The idea of finding an employer truly committed to work-life balance was pretty much out of the question. Any mention of the concept during a job interview would likely be accompanied by an invitation to look elsewhere. Despite protestations to the contrary, companies do not generally accept responsibility for the "balance" employees need in their lives, especially between how much time they devote to work and to private matters. Her mother needed a job whose work schedule fit the lifestyle her new circumstances imposed. Ergo, a work-life "alignment" seemed more practical and appropriate than a "balance." That is, it is not so much that we balance our work and personal time as it is how well those two worlds mesh.

Raising a family as the surviving spouse is difficult under any circumstances. But surviving men usually do not have to resuscitate their careers at the same time. Additionally, men are much less likely than women to have their careers interrupted by conflicting responsibilities and the prolonged absences from the workforce that go along with those pressures. Essentially, life events and cultural expectations impact women's careers much more than men's. Therefore, women's approach to the job market has to be altered accordingly. This chapter takes a look at Rules 1 through 6, with an eye toward those alterations that women need to make, especially when they desire to reenter the job market.

Interrupted Careers

The typical white-collar professional is college educated and career oriented. If he or she is just starting out, the individual has a substantial sense of upward-mobility potential. That is, the current job is viewed as a stepping-stone to other jobs that will eventually carry greater income and prestige. Ambitions would have to be placed on hold if, for whatever reason, the individual needed to leave work for an extended time. But compared to women, men hardly ever consider the possibility that major life decisions, such as having a family, will require that they interrupt their careers. Women routinely understand that a decision to have children carries the corresponding expectations that they may have to put their careers on hold for anywhere from a few months to several years.

Study after study reports that interrupted careers are a cultural expectation for women not generally shared by men. Young, would-be professional women understand that they are more likely to start and restart their careers. And, indeed, many of them do. They enter college and make career decisions with those realities in mind—for example, by choosing careers that have more flexible time commitments, such as college professor versus an attorney in a partnership. Women who ignore these realities risk having to make more difficult choices down the road.

In her senior thesis, Amy Sennett (Princeton class of 2006) concluded that her female classmates seemed as willing as the generations of women before them to "accept the assignment, by biology or society, of child-rearing responsibilities to women." Those responsibilities become more severe when divorce is involved. Most couples do not enter into matrimony with divorce in mind, even though over 50 percent of all marriages end up in divorce. Bob and Ginny recognized that his career had the greatest income potential and hers was secondary—the one that could temporarily be sacrificed when children came along. But two kids and one divorce later, Ginny went from wanting a career to needing one. She felt fortunate in a way because she could rely on Bob to uphold his end of the divorce settlement to support the family's current standard of living.

Yet she suspected that Bob would eventually move on and have another family who would compete for limited resources with the one he left behind. Statistically, Ginny could expect a 27 percent decline in her standard of living, while Bob would experience a 10 percent increase. The difference for Ginny would need to be made up by getting started on the career she had begun and earning the income she gave up for marriage and motherhood.

This situation is not altogether avoided even if the marriage survives. Women are still more likely to get squeezed in the working world because they tend to accept responsibility as primary caregivers for both children and aging parents. That's fine—as long as the spouse remains alive for continued financial support.

After twenty years of marriage, Clarence and Dorothy were confident their union would not be a statistical casualty. Over the years, they were typical of many similarly situated couples in that Dorothy settled in as the primary caregiver for the kids. She tended to stay home when they were sick or other home responsibilities demanded her time. Her boss understood that things were that way, and Clarence never seemed to give the matter a second thought. As the kids grew and

Dorothy and Clarence's parents aged, it seemed natural for Dorothy to lend her caregiving talents to their parents as well. When an absence from work was required, Dorothy was always the natural volunteer.

The toll this took on Dorothy's career came more clearly into focus when Clarence took ill and passed away at what would have been the height of his income-earning years. Initially, she never minded the extended interruptions from work, but now she could have used the extra money that an enhanced career would have provided.

Some career women choose not to get married and/or have children. To complete the picture, however, we see another group of women who decide they can have it all—marriage, children, and a good career, to boot. The latter are today's "supermoms" who are major contributors to their two-income families and whose incomes support a middle- or upper-middle-class standard of living. Plus, these superwomen are often role models for young professional women just entering the workforce.

We have discussed how globalization, technology, and deregulation have changed the rules for finding white-collar work. But these changes have exaggerated impacts on professional women and they call for additional career-management tools. There is good news on the horizon, however. The number of highly educated career women with children has dramatically increased in the past couple of decades. As a result, "on-ramping"—a new term invented to describe women who reenter the workforce, joining the highway traffic of fast-track careers—is creating an entirely new arena of work opportunity. (Its opposite, "off-ramping," describes women who need to exit the career track, perhaps temporarily.) Top business schools such as Wharton, Dartmouth, and Harvard have started programs to accommodate the needs of these high-powered moms. New companies (Mom Corps, Career Partners, Business Talent Group, and others) have come into existence providing companies with high-powered talent on a temporary project basis while meeting the needs mothers have for jobs aligned with their needs.

There are several explanations for this dramatic shift in the employment landscape for women. First, companies and universities need to improve their public relations regarding the special needs of professional women. Second, temporary, or contract, workers are an attractive option for companies because they are less expensive and more flexible (can meet tighter schedules and don't require benefits) than full-timers. Third, tapping into any pool of highly talented workers makes good business sense.

Recent surveys have shown that of the 93 percent of working moms who report wanting to return to the workforce, almost three-quarters are able to do so. The trend is clearly toward increasing flexibility for career women who need to hop on and off the career path. That is, an interrupted career need no longer be synonymous with a ruined career.

That's the good news. The sobering reality is that regardless of where a woman is on the educational ladder she still needs to get into position to take advantage of opportunities. While companies and universities have become more flexible, the basics of the game have not changed. To find suitable white-collar work, you must demonstrate an ability to create value that is aligned with what employers are looking for—and create it in greater abundance than your competitors.

The steps toward creating value have been discussed in earlier chapters, but women need to consider additional factors. Let's look at the steps and see how they apply in the case of an interrupted career.

Value Creation Is the Competitive Edge

Remember Bob, struggling with instability in the workforce? He wondered if employers were beginning to think that the problem was with him and that he simply could not hold a job. He wondered how hiring managers would react to his having had three jobs in five years. Yet Bob found a job in a reasonable amount of time by shifting attention away from issues of workplace stability to highlighting the value he brought to his new position. He accomplished this with a laserlike focus on the value his new employer wanted in a new hire and by linking his past experiences with company requirements.

The image of the on-ramp to the career highway is instructive. Accessing a highway requires a driver to "get up to speed" before merging onto the main road. Going too slow can cause confusion or an accident. But this mistake can be avoided if you remember that *the best way to reenter the job market is to never leave it*. That is, do not allow your career-related activities to lapse, even though you may no longer be an active member of the workforce. Maintain enough speed during that period so that you can merge gracefully with the traffic (the competition).

This rule applies regardless of where you are in your career. If you need an off-ramp, exit in a way that allows you to stay tethered to the job market. You can start the process by choosing a career that allows maximum personal flexibility, but that's not strictly necessary. The key is to keep your value-creation skills sharp and your accomplishments current. There are some practical, easy, and powerful ways to do this.

CONSIDER RETURNING TO SCHOOL

Even if you have an MBA or a Ph.D., you can consider returning to school. You are not after the degree. But returning to school allows you to cherry-pick the curriculum to enhance the skills you already have but may need to improve—and perhaps develop new ones. Skills like project management, public speaking, and computer modeling and analysis are usually good places to start. But attend school to do more than just learn. Try to pick a school that has a strong, highly respected career-placement center. Research the companies that recruit on campus and see where the alumni tend to be employed. Be prepared to contact them and find out as much as you can about these companies and about the job market in general.

Be purposeful when you return to school. Think in terms of doing more than just taking classes. Now is a good time to get to know the professors whose research interests align with yours. Try to take an independent-study course and become involved in the professor's research. Though it may be difficult to get a chance at coauthorship, at least you will be able to list the research on your résumé.

Professors also make for good references and networking contacts. Find out whom they know and whether you can connect with them, very much the way you would when networking. Assess the state of the job market from their perspective, and solicit advice about the best way to reenter it.

CONSIDER VOLUNTEER WORK

A wide variety of not-for-profit organizations can use the skills of the highly educated. Choose an organization that has a particular need in your area of expertise and volunteer your time. Hospitals, religious organizations, community outreach programs, and many others need skillful volunteers.

Judy Carpenter graduated with honors in accounting from her state university and started work as an auditor for a large firm. Before she had a chance to move up in the organization, her career took an off-ramp for the birth of her first child. Rather than return to work immediately, Judy became a stay-at-home mom for three years. Though away from the workforce, she was not inactive. She assumed the duties of chief financial officer (a nonpaying position) for a medium-size charity. She used the experience to broaden her accounting background to include a fuller range of financial management. What she did not know (cash management, tax filings, financial controls, etc.) she picked up through classes at the local community college paid for by her charity. She also solicited the volunteer assistance of several professors who served as on-the-job mentors. Judy's return to work was a relatively easy process that resulted in a promotion from the position she had previously.

TRY TEMPORARY WORK

A temporary assignment should align with other priorities in your life. One of the simplest ways to accomplish this is to contact organizations that specialize in professional women returning to the workforce. These might include Mom Corps, Career Partners, Business Talent Group, and others. These organizations understand the problems involved in restarting a career, and they search for assignments that take work-life alignment into consideration. They also represent "safe" places where women can discuss and learn to manage the anxieties of going back to work.

Your Résumé Is Not About You

Rule #2, "Your Résumé: It's About the Value You Create," is an extensive discussion of how to develop a résumé focused on the value that organizations want when they hire people. You can begin to understand what others want by carefully examining the position descriptions of jobs of interest and for which you would be a viable candidate.

Getting off the fast track is a lot easier than getting back on. Both processes can be highly stressful. You can make reentrance a lot easier if you plan for it as far ahead of time as possible and if you are purposeful in how you do it. The first step is to recognize that the best time to look for work is well before you need to go to work. You should use the "Five Steps to Your Value-Infused Résumé" as a guide during your employment hiatus. Stay in touch with the job market by keeping current on the skills companies are seeking. How do you do that? The same way you prepare your résumé. Understand the value that individual companies are looking to have created when they fill positions. Use the "Key Word" exercise discussed earlier.

1. Identify the key words in the position descriptions of jobs of interest. Also, stay abreast of developments in your field by reading professional journals and articles that describe ongoing issues in the industry or profession. Pay special attention to the words used to describe the issues and the innovative solutions developed to deal with them. This language will be particularly helpful upon reentry.

2. Continue to examine your own experiences in terms of their relevance to new issues that evolve during your absence. Anytime your past experiences seem dated, develop more relevant ones as you return to school, volunteer, or work part-time. This way you can keep up with what is happening in the market and simultaneously keep your skills current. Choose jobs or opportunities that require skills you already have and will be considered a plus by potential employers.

3. Be sure your new skills are attached to substantial accomplishments— co-publishing with a professor, presentations at conferences, volunteer work that results in major organizational gains, and so on. Such achievements demonstrate your ongoing ability to create value.

4. When you are ready to respond to a specific job opportunity, translate the value you have created throughout your career (especially including the hiatus) to the requirements of the position(s) in which you are now interested.

5. We mentioned two types of résumés—chronological and functional— and expressed a strong preference for the former. If you have been out of the job market more than three years, however, a functional résumé may be more appropriate. At a minimum, develop a strongly worded functional career-summary statement to be used as a handbill that highlights your various areas of expertise and accomplishments.

All these strategies may sound like more activity during a break from work than you anticipated. However, you shouldn't have to employ them full-time. From the perspective of career continuity, just make sure no year goes by without value-creation/skill-enhancement activity of some kind. Those who take the time to remain active and career focused will have less trouble restarting their careers compared to those who have big gaps in their résumés.

There Is No Such Thing as the Hidden Job Market

Once you make the decision to go back to work, you may want to know how to reconnect to the "hidden job market." Those strong networking ties you once had probably have not been maintained, and you're not sure you have either the energy or the time to reconnect. The good news is that there isn't any hidden market. Via social networking on the Internet, you can connect with an infinite number of people by establishing weak ties that take less time and are more effective.

There is no general agreement as to the best place or best method that employers use to look for talent. Media advertising is expensive and uncertain; they now broadcast openings in a variety of ways, including the Internet. Numerous groups and blogs allow like-minded people to connect and exchange ideas on the job market. In particular, the matter of on- and off-ramping is currently a hot topic that has attracted professional women at all levels. Establish an Internet presence and develop your personal brand well in advance of returning to work. The effort will be well worth it. Also, now is a good time to experiment with Facebook, LinkedIn, and Twitter.

You can also use the Internet to give a little and get some back. A new group of professional women enters the workforce each year, and many women have the same anxieties and questions you did when you interrupted your career and now as you enter the on-ramp. Very likely, other women could benefit from what you have learned about career management. Perhaps now is a good time to start a blog, or at least join some of the thousands of conversations facilitated by the Internet. Participation is a good way to build your personal brand and Internet presence. Companies interested in your candidacy will be pleased to see other dimensions to your value-creation skills.

The Answers to All Interview Questions Are the Same

You now understand value creation, your résumé is ready for prime time, and you have worked your network for several job leads. You are ready to interview. For a variety of reasons, interviews produce more anxiety than any other stage in the job-search process. This is when you come face-to-face with people who will stand in judgment of your accomplishments and compare them to others'. Understand that it is perfectly normal to be nervous. That's all the more reason to be well prepared. Here is the million-dollar question and corresponding answer:

> **Q:** Why were you out of the workforce so long?
>
> **A:** I am not sure I really ever left. If you look at my credentials closely you will see that I did many things to keep my skills current in anticipation of returning. . . .

Women do not have to apologize for using a career off-ramp and staying there for however long they need. People expect to hear that you have paused to raise your children or care for aging parents. You just need to demonstrate your willingness and ability to create the kind of value employers want when they fill positions.

Reference checks require additional attention. Generally speaking, the longer the period of unemployment, the greater the need to have references that are current. Think of it this way: A reference from a direct supervisor you had fifteen years ago will not have the same impact as more recent experiences. Current references can come from college professors, volunteer organizations, or temporary jobs. Reestablishing a track record is hard work and takes time. That's why you want to plan your reentry as early as possible and start building important relationships well before you want a job. Having to return to work immediately without anything to fill the gap only makes reentry more difficult. Revisit the discussion of references (Rule #4) and follow the suggestions as closely as possible. They are now more important than ever.

PREPARE FOR THE INTERVIEW

This process is especially important. You have been away from work and need to sell yourself more than ever before. Consider this famous joke: A tourist asks someone on the street, "How do I get to Carnegie Hall?" The person responds, "Practice, practice, practice."

That punch line is the correct answer to the question of how to prepare for an interview, especially when you have been absent from the workplace. Don't memorize the answers to a bunch of theoretical questions that may never be asked. Plus, some of your answers will have to be developed on the spur of the moment. If you are well prepared, you'll able to give extemporaneous answers to unanticipated questions.

You'll recognize the opportunity to talk about things of interest to the employer and relate them to your experiences when the opportunity presents itself. Identify the key words in the position description of the job for which you are applying. Visit the company's website and pay close attention to industry publications. Once you know what is of interest to a potential employer, and have identified related experiences from your work history, begin to formulate questions an interviewer might ask. Then practice, practice, and practice. And remember, the answers to all interview questions should be treated as opportunities to talk about topics of interest to the employer.

STANDARD TOUGH QUESTIONS

Aside from the question of what you've been doing during the hiatus, which have been covered, the toughest question you probably will face is that of salary. Have a salary amount in mind but do not reveal it. Conduct a computer search on what people in your field with your experience are paid. Companies generally like to leave room for merit increases and midyear adjustments, if warranted. That is more difficult when they start someone at the top rather than the bottom of a salary range. Also, keep in mind that companies are loath to overpay. If a search consultant is involved, you can use the individual to probe salary issues, but don't count on him or her to gauge how competitive a salary offer is compared with that of other firms; search agents work for the company and have the company's best interests in mind during this stage of the job-search process.

When a salary offer is forthcoming, remember that you and the company already agree on the most important things—you want a job and it wants to offer you one. If the salary is absolutely below what you need to survive financially, you may want to turn the job down. Most people, however, don't find themselves in that situation. Usually, you'll want more money without being sure if more money is justified. When you have a sense of the market, you have a better idea of whether it is a good offer or not.

Interviewers are advised to steer clear of questions about conflicts between home responsibilities and work because they too easily stray into areas that are inappropriate and even illegal to inquire about. The arrangements you need to make at home during work time are your business. The presumption should be that those have little or nothing to do with the job. However, here's how to handle the matter, should it arise:

Q. Do you have emergency day-care support so you can be here if needed?

A. I have never had any problems managing my work and personal life.

Keep the answer short so as not to invite further intrusion. Do not offer details about your life unrelated to the job, including the arrangements required for you to meet a demanding work schedule. Think of such questions this way: Would a man be asked the same question? If a man with a family doesn't have to answer them, why should a woman have to? In addition, any details you provide about how you would manage the situation at home to respond to a work emergency will only invite further questions.

You Get What You Negotiate, Not What You Deserve

Given the special issues women face, Rule #5 has a few additional wrinkles. The list of things you want in your next job, how they are prioritized, and how to use them in negotiations are particularly important. A typical list of priorities for a new job in middle management might be as follows:

Must-Haves

▸ Work-life alignment

▸ No more than 20 percent travel

- Three weeks' vacation

- Bonus opportunity (40 percent)

Would Like to Have

- No relocation

- 401 company match (25 percent)

- Effective career-development programs

- Company car

Want, but Can Do Without

- Pay raise over last job

- Competitive employee contribution to medical plan

- Immediate coverage for preexisting conditions

The list says a lot about existing priorities. Yet it is okay for your list of priorities to be flexible. If someone in the family suddenly developed a serious illness, coverage of preexisting conditions would move to the "must-have" category. The purpose of the list is to determine what is important to you and what trade-offs may be necessary.

The preference for "work-life alignment" is of particular interest here because you need to define the situation more closely. The more general the terms, the greater the room for misunderstanding. You should be clear in your own mind precisely what these terms mean to you in everyday work situations. Expecting flexibility occasionally to deal with emergencies is quite different from expecting it week after week or day after day.

Flexible work hours mean different things in different companies—and even in different departments within the same company. If you need flexibility, ask to see a copy of the company's policy on flexible work arrangements. If no policy exists, flexibility is usually negotiated on a case-by-case basis. You should regard this as the first sign of an unhealthy situation because every time you have a change in immediate supervisor you may have to renegotiate your flexible work arrangement. Contrast this to companies such as IBM, which have employees around the globe who work from home and are covered by a formal policy.

Generally speaking, in the absence of a policy covering flexible work arrangements, you should be specific about the details of the flexibility you need and have it put in writing. Penning a memorandum to your boss can be justified as "your attempt to make sure you heard the discussion correctly." Avoid legalese and any appearance that the memo is being written as a CYA document. Reducing an agreement to writing is a good way to make sure both parties heard each other correctly and are operating with the same set of assumptions. It will give you time to correct any misunderstandings before they surface in other ways.

Remember, do not negotiate your working conditions too soon. Current employees are the best barometer of how a company really works vis-à-vis flexible work hours and other aspects of employment particularly important to professional women. Before any negotiations, get the lay of the land by speaking with as many similarly situated women as possible.

The period of time between when an offer is formally made and when you accept is the time to negotiate. You have more bargaining power than at any other time. Closure on the deal is near at hand, save perhaps for a few details that should be easy to negotiate.

Of the seven rules for skillful negotiation, two in particular deserve additional emphasis: underplay your hand, and underpromise and overdeliver. Underplaying your hand is a reminder to avoid haggling over relatively unimportant details. You already have a list of priorities you want in a new job. Many of the items should be flexible and able to move from one category to another as the negotiation goes forward. If an item is nonnegotiable, it may be cause for walking away from the opportunity.

Underpromising and overdelivering requires a shift in mindset that can be extremely difficult, especially after you are most of the way up the on-ramp. Just remember: if you follow this rule, you will be regarded as a high achiever who understands the complexities of challenging assignments and who excels when it comes to delivering on your promises.

• • • • • • • • • • *Things to Remember* • • • • • • • • •

▸ *Women routinely expect their careers will be interrupted by the cultural expectations of motherhood and caregiving.*

▸ *The road to career success is more difficult for women than men.*

▸ *Companies are largely unsympathetic to the needs people have for work-life balance. The challenge becomes one of finding work structured in a way to allow work-life alignment.*

▸ *The employment landscape has improved for highly educated professional women. To take advantage requires careful planning.*

▸ *If you need use of an off-ramp, remember to stay tethered to the job market. Keep your value creation skills current.*

▸ *Make reentry plans as far ahead of when you want to return to work as possible. Remember, the best way to reenter the job market is to never leave it.*

NOTE

1. Allison O'Kelly, CEO, Mom Corps, personal interview, July 6, 2010.

Helicopter Parenting Is a Good Thing

WHAT SHOULD parents do to prepare their children for a work environment that is more volatile and challenging than ever? That question is on the minds of a lot of people because of the strong possibility that current trends toward job and career instability will continue. It would be great if our kids could inherit a world in which college was affordable, jobs were abundant, and career paths were always onward and upward.

Of course, that world no longer exists. More and more these days, second mortgages are routinely needed to finance college educations, a college degree is no longer an automatic ticket to white-collar work, and many careers are vanishing in the global restructuring of the workforce.

A number of observers argue that the financial return on a college education is not worth the cost, especially for the almost 50 percent who will enter as freshmen and never finish. That conclusion seems too radical. Most parents will not abandon their commitment to a college education for their children. The types of jobs remaining in the United States require a higher level of education. Certainly, college administrators agree with parents and encourage them to stay the course. They are not, though, disinterested parties in the debate.

Higher Education as a Vocational Stepping-Stone

For the past several decades the message from college and university administrators has been that education pays. The higher the degree, the better. As evidence, they point out that lifetime earnings for those with bachelor's degrees are nearly twice the earnings of those with high school diplomas. Furthermore, people with master's, doctorates, and professional degrees show a steady progression upward of lifetime earnings. These studies are not just endorsed by colleges and universities; they serve as a first line of defense against complaints that higher education costs are too high and have risen too quickly—faster than either the cost of living or earnings of the general population.

The trends have been consistent for the past six decades as students continue to flock to college in greater numbers. More education is the ready answer to fulfilling one's career ambitions. The message to high school students is, "If you want to make something of yourself, go to college." This message piggybacks an already existing mindset—easy to believe and relatively easy to execute as billions of dollars are made available through private and government-backed loan programs. It plays out as a mad frenzy among many of the nation's colleges and universities to recruit their fair share of students and the tuitions they pay.

As a result, colleges and universities are no longer simply benign institutions performing a public service. Higher education has itself become big business—so much so that the most significant growth sector in higher education is among for-profit colleges that now educate more than 7 percent of the nation's 19 million students. Phoenix University, the largest among them, has an enrollment of over 455,000 students, a population larger than the entire undergraduate enrollment of the Big Ten. And student recruiting budgets continue to grow in proportion.

Each year more than 78 percent of high school students say they would like to go to college—a number that is consistently high across most racial and ethnic minorities as well. When it comes to faith in higher education, most of us are true believers.

That places parents under the gun. The conversation around Bruce and Dora Miller's Seattle dinner table was like many others. They discussed the financial adjustments necessary to send both of their children to the private colleges of their choice. Like over 50 percent of the respondents in a national poll, they concluded that the only way they could do it would be to postpone retirement and take on a second mortgage. Even a majority of those who thought they could afford to send their kids to college also reported that they would have to make deep cuts in their discretionary spending.

They are expecting a return on their investment. That's because businesses for many years accepted the college degree as the credential for entry into their white-collar jobs. On that same survey, more than 75 percent of high school seniors say they want to attend college for vocational reasons. That is, they want to qualify for a good job.

But the rules have changed. The correlation between a college degree and a white-collar job is becoming more tenuous. College degrees are now commonplace: today's bachelor's degree is the equivalent of yesterday's high school diploma. College graduates are still able to find work, but many jobs do not pay enough to allow students to live away from home and service their student debt at the same time. At the height of the Great Recession, more than 40 percent of recent college grads reported still living at home. The phenomenon is so widespread that the term "boomerang children" was invented. Rather than "Go to college and get a job," the new refrain is, "Now that I have my degree, where is my career?"

This situation has given rise to another set of conversations in American households. John Patterson's college degree was made possible by a combination of financial support from his parents and student loans. A year after graduation and still making little more than minimum wage, he asked his parents for an extension of his rent-free living arrangement with them until his financial situation improved. Like so many others, John's parents were sympathetic. But they wondered in private how much of John's situation was caused by the economy and how much was John's fault—his choice of major and his grade point average. They couldn't tell, so they stayed the course. With unemployment holding at 9.5 percent, many people were having trouble finding any job at all.

But if you think you can relax once the Great Recession ends, think again. Jobs will continue to move beyond national boundaries as the worldwide restructuring of the workforce continues and competition for white-collar jobs becomes even more intense. The message bears repeating. A healthy economy will not change the underlying dynamics of the global marketplace. Globalization has caused competition for all kinds of work—including white-collar jobs—to escalate.

Parents (and students) are left with an unanswered question: What will a college degree do for my son's or daughter's career? The answer is the new linkages between careers and higher education—how they work and what you can do to make them work for your child. The time has passed when a parent can blindly rely on the belief that a college degree also confers a middle-class income to its recipient.

Many colleges haven't changed their mission, however, or their view of linkages between higher education and career opportunity. A director of career services at one of the nation's most prestigious universities typified how universities are programmed to respond when she commented:

> [The] concern was echoed recently by a group of guidance counselors from across the country who visited [my] University. I asked them to tell me the number one concern of parents. Unanimously, they asserted that parents wanted their children to use their education experience to obtain a successful career.

As a parent, I understand this concern. After all, college often costs enough to require a second mortgage. As director of a large career center, however, I know that parents often worry unnecessarily. That is because I've seen plenty of philosophy majors who've managed to do everything from investment banking to law to starting their own business. Marshall Gregory, professor of English, liberal education and pedagogy at Butler University puts it this way. "In 35 years of teaching, I have never seen a student who really wanted a job fail to get one after graduation. . . . But I have seen many students fail to get an education because they were fixated on the fiction that one particular major or another held the magical key to financial success for the rest of their lives." For guidance counselors, there is a real balance between encouraging the educational aspirations of students and assuaging the fears of their parents.[1]

In fairness, the comments were not intended to explain how your child can make the transition from philosophy major to business magnate. But the comments are clearly more comforting to administrators than to either parents or students. Parents continue to be told that if the student really wants a good job he or she can get one. In other words, the message is, "When it comes to your child's career, trust us. It will all work out in the end if the student really wants it to." The reasoning, of course, is completely circular. If it doesn't work out, the student didn't really want it to.

Such blind faith may have been justified when college degrees were not so plentiful and companies were scrambling for a fair share of graduating college seniors. The scenario has changed dramatically, however, especially if a parent has to take out a second mortgage or a student takes on substantial student loans. Parents and students alike would be more comfortable taking on debt to attend institutions whose administrators promise that their university understands the connection between educational attainment and career management and is committed to making that a key component of what each student learns during his or her time there. But according to longstanding tradition, the curriculum is the province of the faculty, which appropriately refuses to allow their educational content to be hijacked so that their college serves as a vocational clearinghouse for students.

As such, a disconnect has developed between the reasons many students go to college and what most colleges are prepared to deliver. Parents and students alike must look elsewhere for vocational direction. Just before his freshman year, John Patterson had a detailed discussion with his parents about what he might choose as a major and what his job prospects would be. Their collective sense was that the next four years would be a time of growing independence from each other and John would gradually assume control for his choices ahead of him. They trusted that the university had enough resources and experience to steer John in the right direction. In retrospect, they wondered if their trust was justified.

Those experiences are surprisingly typical. Consider this: Two sociologists recently tracked 2,300 students through four years of college. After two years, they reviewed what students were learning in the way of critical thinking, complex reasoning, and written communication—all skill improvement areas appropriate to an undergraduate education regardless of academic major. The answer they got was students were learning "little or nothing." Of the 60 percent who had full-time jobs after graduation, more than two-thirds were making less than $35,000 and an astonishing 45 percent were earning $15,000 or less.[2]

Parents Need to Hover More

Perhaps you have heard of "helicopter parenting." Coined in the early 1990s, it is a pejorative term used to describe those who are overly involved in the lives of their college-age children. Some stories have reached legendary status. For example, one college freshman handed her cell phone to a university administrator so she could explain to the student's mother why a class was no longer available. Another parent went to see a professor to let him know that the grade his son received was not what he needed to get into graduate school.

Fervent helicopter parents know no boundaries when it comes to advancing the interests of their children. When their behavior crosses certain ethical lines, they are dubbed "Black Hawks." These are parents who write papers for their children or otherwise endorse getting the desired result at all cost.

A commonly accepted explanation of the rise of helicopter parents is that they are baby-boomer moms and dads determined to micromanage every aspect of their children's lives. One sociologist quoted in the *St. Petersburg Times* commented that the fault lies with parents who "saw their youngsters as special and sheltered them. Parents outfitted their cars with Baby-on-Board stickers. They insisted their children wear bicycle helmets, knee pads and elbow guards. They led the PTA and developed best-friend like relationships with their children."[3] These parents reportedly call their children to wake them for class and expect daily progress reports.

The involvement of parents has spilled off the campus and into the workplace. Parents now call employers to negotiate salary offers and attend interviews. Some employers have acquiesced and invited parents to job-fair open houses to give them a firsthand view of their employment process.

College administrators take a dim view of helicopter parents, encouraging them to step back and give their children a chance to learn life's lessons on their own. They claim, "If they don't grow up now, they never will." In fact, the term "helicopter parent" was invented—or at least popularized—by university administrators.

That is grounds for suspicion. No group should be given a free pass in characterizing individuals who make their lives uncomfortable. Rather than examine the overindulgence of a generation of parents, more satisfying answers would be found by examining the overindulgence of higher education itself.

Higher education has, on balance, never felt compelled to take a student's future career into consideration in the normal operation of its business. Campus administrators responsible for job placement usually do not take part in the decision making of the institutions in which they serve, in spite of the fact that they represent that part of the university most responsive to what students attend college to get. Placement-center personnel desperately need to upgrade their craft but have neither the resources nor the work experience beyond the university to do so. Colleges and universities accepted the revenue from career-driven student demand for higher education without fully accepting the responsibility. When seen in this light, helicopter parents are filling a role that has gained urgency as the world of work has changed.

The behavior of helicopter parents can be explained, in part, by a reversal of fortune from more white-collar jobs than degreed students to one of more students than jobs. The worldwide restructuring of the workforce will continue to aggravate the situation as competition for white-collar work takes on a growing international dimension. Who would have thought a few years ago that IBM would have 50,000 employees (15 percent of its employee population) located in Bangalore, India?

Insulated to a large degree from these concerns, colleges have been slow to move beyond the traditional "trust us" response. A college president recently asked, "Whatever happened to the days when Mom and Dad dropped you off at college—maybe helped you with moving in—and left for home hoping to hear from you once a week (on Sunday) and planning to see you next at Thanksgiving?"

We can now answer that question. Those days disappeared when parents began to realize that higher education was costing more and delivering less on the far end. Parents have stepped in because they are unsure what their child will do after college.

Over time, higher education will have to respond more aggressively to the vocational aspirations of students. But the job your child needs after college does not happen over time—it happens now and in the near future.

Filling a Void

Once the freshman year begins, you will have difficulty getting the attention of your college-age children concerning certain subjects. Career planning tends to be one of them because it doesn't have the sense of immediacy for freshmen that it will command down the road. Students get busy meeting new friends and basking in the glow of independent living away from Mom and Dad.

But as parents, you know graduation is right around the corner. Don't wait for their senior year, when the prospect of postgraduate unemployment sends students scrambling to the campus's career services center for guidance. A major reason they are attending college is to qualify for a job that pays well and has career potential.

Your job, in part, will be to make sure your child is career ready. As it stands, far too many students are in a mad scramble late in their senior year to find a job. They will want to interview with companies that visit campus each year in search of talent. They will go online to find everything from résumé templates to companies that hire students with their major and grade point average. Some students will be able to list summer jobs and travel abroad on their résumés as evidence they have taken their undergraduate years seriously. But that may not be enough to convince employers they are among the best of this year's graduating crop. Most students look just like the many thousands of other graduating seniors with indistinguishable résumés and backgrounds.

Parents can urge their child to choose a major that is in demand in the job market. Engineering, economics, and business are usually preferred over philosophy, English, and women's studies. Some students know exactly what they want to do and follow a course of action that delivers upon graduation. Others are not so sure. Regardless, there is no reason for any student to ignore that finding a good job that leads to a solid career is a primary motivator for initially going to college.

How pleased would you be if the assessment of recruiters was that your graduating college senior "clearly represents the kind of person we look to hire"? That is the assessment of an elite group every year. You would be surprised to know they are not always the smartest or have the highest GPAs. It makes you wonder, "What do they know that we don't?"

First, parents should understand that they need to be more, not less, involved when their children are in college. That is, they need to be more like those helicopter parents who understand that the time has passed when college is merely a way station between adolescence and adulthood. College shouldn't be all work and no play. But career management does demand attention and planning. And parents can help.

Some, like the Pattersons, wanted to be involved but were unsure how to go about it. Most people feel attending interviews or writing term papers is beyond the limits. But every time you think you know where the boundary line is, it moves. Take, for example, the idea of paying cash so your son or daughter can work. Who in their right mind would pay someone to hire your kid? Yet a growing number of parents have warmed to the idea of paying between $6,000 and $9,500 for unpaid internships for their children.

That is the idea behind the for-profit company University of Dreams. Sound hokey? Think again. It advertises itself as the "premier provider of summer internships for college students" and boasts of partnerships with over 3,500 employers. Its website has a special page devoted to parents, where it says, in essence, what placement center directors cannot: it will make providing a link between college and career management a key component of what each student learns during his or her time with the company. In other words, it is stepping into a void that was left by the changing marketplace of jobs.

The company proceeds to embed the vocational aspirations of students into a curriculum that is unencumbered by the traditional concerns of an academic faculty. The pitch to parents includes:

10+ years of experience placing students

10,000+ student participants

99 percent placement rate

Over 5,000 internship opportunities at any one time

Another for-profit company, Fast Track Internships, has stepped into the breach as well. It offers three money-back-guaranteed levels of service: unpaid and paid internships and at least two job interviews. These services are available for $800, $1,000, and $2,000, respectively.

Would a company really hire someone whose parents paid for an internship? Such "jobs" seem little more than "silver spoons" for well-to-do parents trying to buy success for their children rather than have them earn it. In reality, it is an inexpensive way for companies to get a close look at potential employees. When they see an intern they like, the decision to hire is easy. Companies tend to prefer students with work experience—especially internships—and generally do not care how the experience is financed.

Some critics of paid internships argue that they are yet another perk that favors the well-off at the expense of the poor. Others cannot get used to the idea of paying to hire their kid solely for the purpose of gaining experience. Further, the requirement to spend additional monies appears as a cruel hoax for parents with second mortgages and students laboring under the weight of educational loans. But the growing popularity of parent-paid internships underscores the competitiveness of the global white-collar job market, the reluctance of colleges to deliver a vocationally based service, and the need companies have to select the best candidates as economically as possible.

Value Creation in the Ivory Tower

You don't have to pay for internships, but you can take action during the college years. Now is not the time for parents to withdraw and let students learn life's lessons on their own. Here are three steps that can help you create your own linkage:

1. Get additional information that can be used to help you understand the lay of the land.

2. Make college experiences count—develop a plan of attack.

3. Help your children translate the plan into actionable items during the course of their time at college.

Additional Information

Is the choice of college major important? It is, but in a way that is different from how you might expect. Let's face it: employers who come to campus looking for accountants or engineers are not likely to interview philosophy majors. And every parent's nightmare is that his or her son or daughter will choose a major that is totally disconnected from what campus recruiters want to see. However, parental reasoning on the subject is flawed on two accounts. First, those graduating with highly sought-after degrees are no less subject to the vagaries of the job market than others. Though it may appear easier for some majors to find employment immediately after college, their jobs get downsized and outsourced at rates similar to others—and, in the case of some majors, even faster. Graduating engineers, for example, are often dismayed at how quickly their skills become obsolete and how willing employers are to move engineering jobs elsewhere. Likewise, MBAs from prestigious universities are not spared when a company downsizes. Being highly sought after immediately following graduation can give a graduate a false sense of security, making the fall back to reality after a downsizing more painful.

Parents are quick to point out that facing the prospect of losing a job is better than having no job at all. If your children are among the fortunate few who know exactly what career they want and the college major that matches, they should go for it. But do not be dismayed if your kids do not fit that pattern.

Second, the choice of college major isn't nearly as important as you might think. There are plenty of entry-level jobs for those who qualify. The qualifications for those positions depend more on the characteristics and skills an applicant brings to the table than on a college major. For example, of the top fifty companies conducting on-campus interviews, only 35 percent report college major as being most important. A whopping 65 percent look first at other characteristics that are not specific to a particular major, and a very significant 45 percent are interested first and foremost in soft skills such as leadership, decision making, writing, and presentation skills. Further, only 5 percent mentioned grade point average. While you should encourage your children to study hard and choose a "good" major, their refusal need not have disastrous career consequences.

That's because the type of degree doesn't matter as much as the value an applicant learns to create. Each year employers have to make a "guesstimate" as to which students will create the value they demand—that is, which of them has the greatest potential and therefore represents the best investment opportunity. You will be surprised to know that these are often liberal arts majors. What they often lack, however, is a specific understanding of how to convert their academic preparation into value for companies recruiting on campus.

Make Experiences Count

Jobs most often go to those who are able to match up what the student has accomplished during his or her time in college with what employers value. If seen in this respect, a freshman has four years to demonstrate his or her relevance to the job market. If you allow your child to treat college as a way station, the time will pass without significant vocational progress. That can be avoided by developing a plan of attack.

Meanwhile, parents should remember that choosing a major can be an emotional experience. It usually means that a chord of intellectual curiosity has been struck and a student wants to pursue a specific subject he or she is interested in. It is unnecessarily discouraging when that choice is challenged by parents and friends with no other thought in mind except whether a job awaits at the end. Good jobs are available for college graduates with majors unattractive to their parents. The student just has to demonstrate the ability to create value.

A Plan of Attack

Think about the issue of employment after college as a job search even if your child is unsure about what he or she wants to do. Do not allow indecision about career choice to stand in the way of developing a relevant skill set. Your child has four years to develop the profile he or she needs to be perceived as a strong candidate for many entry-level positions regardless of major.

Where do you get the information that tells you what companies want? The same place you would if you were looking for a job. You read position descriptions. Before your son or daughter goes off to school for the freshman year, call or visit your placement center with your child and ask to see examples of typical position descriptions companies use when they recruit on campus. If your child is unsure what he or she wants to major in, ask for position descriptions for jobs that do not require a specific major.

You will find many characteristics in common whether a major is specified or not. Almost all employers would like to see evidence of leadership, computer, writing, analytical, and communication skills. You might also discover a preference for students who have had internships and good grade point averages. Share this information with your child and ask, "What do you need to do over the next four years to demonstrate you have developed those skills over and above others against whom you will compete?" This same question needs to be asked at the beginning and end of every year in school as a measure of progress.

Next, revisit the discussion regarding Rule #2 under "Five Steps to Your Value-Infused Résumé." It will help both of you to think of how you will eventually make connections between your child's experiences (during and before college) and the value employers look for employees to create. The five steps were initially intended to help the reader develop a focused résumé. When employers come across a résumé focused on the value they want created, it piques their interest. The same is true for entry-level positions. Students who have tailored their experiences in college to directly address the requirements of employers will stand a better chance of quality employment.

As a reminder, those five steps are repeated here with appropriate modifications:

1. Identify key words in the position descriptions that indicate what employers consider to be of value. This does not preclude you or your child from opting out. If your child does not want to gain the kinds of experiences asked for, that's not the right job for him or her. But make that decision intentional rather than accidental.

2. Direct your child in listing experiences as he or she makes the four-year journey through college. Your child probably will not use all the experiences for each position of interest. But he or she will be in a good position to pick and choose which ones fit best with what a given employer seeks.

3. Infuse those experiences with value through a process of qualification and quantification. That is, the emphasis should be on accomplishments and not just activity.

4. Select the best statements when the time comes. This should be done throughout the college years as your child applies for various opportunities.

It's good practice and will enhance the chances of successfully competing for jobs and internships throughout college.

5. Format your experiences. That is, put a résumé together right now based on jobs your child might eventually apply for or be interested in. This could be a difficult exercise, but it will help all concerned see the gaps and provide focus on bridging them.

This may well be a difficult discussion to have with your children. That should not deter you from providing them with a firsthand understanding of the process. If you run up against an adolescent wall, try to discuss piecemeal the more specific issues listed in the next section.

You should remember that developing a relevant skill set does not mean urging your children to ignore activities unrelated to a future job search. College is also a great time to study the arts and literature, and other topics of aesthetic interest. Just make sure that some of what they do every year helps to build a personal profile that will make sense to employers.

Focus on Action

Planning for the future may be too vague a concept to interest your children. You may need a more concrete translation of what the plan means. Worry less about major and GPA (though do not ignore them altogether) and concentrate on action steps once they reach campus. Here is a list of possible options written as though they are directions provided from parent to child. This may help you find the right words.

▶ *Survive.* Making the adjustment to college is not easy, and over 25 percent of all students leave before the freshman year has ended. The various reasons include too much party time, loneliness, poor academic preparation, the wrong courses, money, and generally being overwhelmed. Recognize when you are in danger of not surviving and get help. Before the freshman year starts, let's find out from university representatives why students drop out and what resources are available on campus to help.

▶ *Think small.* You want to create the kind of value in your extracurricular activities that employers will find attractive. Pick a small activity or club that piques your interests or holds relevance to a potential career option and join early. Why? Because in a small club you will have a greater opportunity to demonstrate the results employers can relate to as factors in succeeding in their own jobs. In a small club, your contribution becomes magnified and the leadership responsibility you can hold early on is significantly greater than in a large organization. At this stage of your development, employers will place emphasis on how well you did something and not so much on what you did.

Thinking small not only applies to extracurricular activities but also to classes. Small classes give you an opportunity to get to know professors better and thereby gain experiences that create value. The best way to determine which professors you should target is to read their CVs to find out their research interests, books and papers they have written, and their previous experience in their field of expertise. When you find a professor whose interests marry with yours, attempt to develop a relationship by taking one of his or her small classes, attending his or her office hours, and signing up for independent study with that professor. Getting to know one or two professors well has added advantages. They may become potential networking contacts, and/or they may give you an opportunity to undertake research and analytical experiences that are valued by today's employers.

▶ *Learn to communicate more effectively.* The Job Outlook report, published annually by the National Association of Companies and Employers (NACE), consistently reports that the ability to speak and write clearly is the number-one skill employers are looking for in entry-level applicants. Yet it is the number-one skill that is most often absent.

Perfecting your communication skills is of utmost importance. Any value created is value obscured if it cannot be communicated. Students should hone their writing skills by taking elective writing classes and getting published. You may wonder, "How in the world can someone in college get published unless that person is the next coming of Hemingway?" Actually, it is much easier than you think. Numerous college journals, department publications, and countless other organizations regularly publish articles, memos, newsletters, and reports, and they actively seek student submissions.

Public-speaking classes, which almost all colleges offer, are a great way to polish verbal-communication skills. Additionally, students should seek opportunities to present speeches at symposiums and research seminars. Almost all academic departments offer these opportunities to interested students, and being able to highlight these on a résumé is a great way to underscore a commitment to value creation.

▶ *Get connected.* Conventional wisdom has it that the only way to network one's way to a job is through a well-established set of networking relationships. Weak networking ties work just as well and probably better. Research by sociologist Mark Granovetter found that almost 60 percent of people who find jobs through networking actually do so through weak ties. They have the added advantage of being easier to establish and maintain as compared with strong ones. In addition, the person you connect with is as important as the strength of the tie. Connect with people who know many others who are connected to the kinds of opportunities you want (these people are called connectors). Weak ties with one or two very well-connected people (think small) works better than plowing inordinate amounts of time trying to cultivate strong ties with ten people.

Oftentimes the best networks (and the ones students most readily neglect) are parents—the parents of their roommates, parents of friends, and many other adults including professors. These people have more experience and are often willing to help out a college student in need.

▶ *Land that intern job.* Paid internships work for some people but not for others. The fewer resources you have, the more you should think small. Where a student works doesn't matter as much as the value he or she creates while working there. That is what employers will focus on. The important thing is not so much what you do but the value you create while doing it! Participation is not enough. Focus on actually accomplishing something.

Start Sooner Rather Than Later

The time to start teaching your children the power of value creation is sooner than you might think. Our work with the KIPP Academy in New York City is a case in point. KIPP is a national network of over fifty-seven college-preparatory public schools in underresourced communities serving more than 14,000 students. Started in 1994, by Mike Feinberg and Dave Levin, in Houston, Texas, after they completed their commitments to Teach For America, KIPP has a student population that is of over 90 percent African-American and Hispanic-Latino descent. Yet 80 percent of KIPP alumni go to college. A value-creation method was designed to help KIPPsters graduating from college to connect to the job market. The program was needed because KIPP students were just like others who, upon graduation from college, were beginning to ask, "Now that I have my degree, where is my career?" They needed to distinguish themselves in a crowded job market. Again, understand that work experiences for KIPP students happen once they leave KIPP and move on to high school and college.

KIPP New York is a middle school in the Bronx that uses work experiences as a primary means for helping students understand the world of work. The KIPP-to-College counseling staff asked us to put together a program for use in determining the kinds of experiences students would need to be competitive upon graduation from college. Essentially, KIPP students leave middle school after the eighth grade but remain tethered to KIPP through job placement and counseling support through college. The objective was to supplement the job-placement activity and provide a broader understanding of jobs and the organizations in which they worked. This was accomplished by requiring each student to fill out a questionnaire during the course of each job. We asked them questions about:

- What the organization does

- How it services its customers

- The value created by the organization

- How the value they create is measured

- What the various jobs are within the organization

- Who some of the most important workers are

- What the most significant thing is that the student can do to contribute to the value the organization creates

By the time a student is ready to enroll in college, he or she has been exposed to the larger picture of how organizations work, why companies look for specific kinds of talent, and what experiences students need to be competitive in the job market. The program lays the groundwork for understanding value creation.

> • • • • • • • • • • **Things to Remember** • • • • • • • • •
>
> ▶ *Higher education is now a big business, and demand for it is driven by the will-ingness of companies to accept the college degree as the ticket of entry to white-collar jobs.*
>
> ▶ *Over 75 percent of students say they attend college for vocational reasons—that is, to be eligible for a good job. Universities have for years accepted the revenue from vocationally driven demand for higher education without accepting the voca-tion aspect of the responsibility.*
>
> ▶ *"Trust us" that your son's or daughter's career will work out fine is no longer acceptable in light of college costs. The college degree is now the equivalent of a high school diploma and no longer guarantees a middle-class lifestyle.*
>
> ▶ *Parents need to be more, not less, involved once their kids go off to college. They can become involved by helping them prepare for their college years the same way someone prepares for a job search.*
>
> ▶ *College major and GPA are not nearly as important as value creation. What stu-dents major in doesn't matter as much as what they learn to do with whatever degree they have.*

NOTES

1. See Sheila Curran, "Choosing a Major or Concentration," June 6, 2008, http://curranoncareers.com/choosing-a-major-or-concentration/.

2. Amanda M. Fairbanks, "College's Value Added," *New York Times,* January 7, 2011.

3. Shannon Colavecchio-Van Sickler, "Mommy, Tell My Professor He's Not Nice," *St. Petersburg Times,* June 19, 2009.

Financial Planning for New Career Realities

ACCORDING TO THE National Bureau of Economic Research, the Great Recession officially began in December 2007. Ordinary citizens, however, felt its effects long before, as factories closed, unemployment rose, and the housing market took a tumble surpassing the dot-com bubble burst in the first few years of the new millennium. The Great Recession has been by far the most severe downturn since the Great Depression, and it has caused comparable levels of economic trauma. A look at that era provides another instructive example. The decade immediately preceding the Great Depression, the "Roaring Twenties," was a time of conspicuous consumption that came to an abrupt end in 1929. Sound familiar? Well, that depression fundamentally changed the consumption patterns of Americans for the next forty years.

Research done by Deloitte and Harrison Group presented a compelling case that "years of keeping up with the Joneses, spending beyond limits, and a tolerance for wastage also seem to have come to an end,"[1] just as it did following the Great Depression, and the changes are likely to last for several generations as well.

The message throughout this book has been that if you want to find work, manage your career, and help your children with their careers, you must know that the job-hunt rules have changed. In a different time and under different circumstances people thought of the financial planning they did after they had been laid off as "contingency planning." That was when white-collar terminations were rare and contingency planning was optional. Today, we must stay on our toes at all times. Careers don't last a lifetime, and jobs sometimes don't last long enough for the ink on the offer letter to dry. How someone manages his or her financial affairs requires close attention and careful planning.

This new urgency applies especially to married white-collar couples. They are mostly two-income families with an unprecedented ability to take on debt. For them, job loss can be doubly damaging. For instance, Tim and Doris felt good about their careers. Married five years with one child, and a combined income of $130,000, they were living the American dream. Their college degrees had paid handsome dividends. So they were sick and tired of the continual nagging from Tim's parents about the importance of financial planning and the warnings that they had taken on too much debt. The advice frequently came in the form of irritating "conventional wisdoms" from what seemed like ages ago. "My dad grew up during the Depression," Tim's father would begin, "and he always reminded us that it was not how much you make—it's how much you spend."

From Tim's perspective, their cash flow easily allowed them to meet monthly obligations. They wondered if his mom and dad were just jealous of their lifestyle. Then disaster struck. Their worst nightmare took the form of successive notifications from their respective employers that their jobs were scheduled for elimination. An MBA provided no protection against downsizing.

They quickly saw that their monthly financial obligations would overwhelm the limited funds they had available. The mortgage payment alone took up most of one of the paychecks. Then they had two car payments, high credit-card debt, a bill consolidation loan, and other monthly "necessities" just to live. Their intent all along had been to do some serious financial planning. Now they were in scramble mode.

Prudence and better financial planning would have helped them avoid their predicament. That story can be multiplied thousands of times around the country. The American consumer is in the midst of a sea change with respect to white-collar jobs and the financial benefits that come with them. Americans have begun to tighten their belts, change their consumption habits, and generally prepare for a very different kind of economic future. It makes sense for you to do the same. You can start by coming to grips with the reality that sound financial planning and career management consider workforce instability as a matter of course now. In this brave new world, the value you learn to create becomes the bridge to your next job opportunity. This is a much easier journey if you have sufficient cash on hand while you cross.

Financial Planning

First, understand that this section is not about how to invest. "Financial planning," according to Ken Little, a well-respected personal financial planner, "is nothing more than being very intentional about how you spend, save and invest."[2] While this has a lot in common with career management, the objective here is much simpler, and in many respects more immediately useful.

Most people understand the need to do some form of financial planning but they put it off. They make it a priority only when there is a pending event (the birth of a child, applying for a mortgage) or an imminent crisis (loss of one's job). Parental reaction to the skyrocketing cost of college is a case in point. When asked, most people say they intend to pay for their children to attend college. Yet a full majority do not set aside sufficient funds to make that happen.

Saving for retirement suffers from the same shortsightedness. We know we should plan, but most of us do not save at a rate that will allow us to retire at our preretirement standard of living. Long-range planning simply isn't as urgent as the next month's rent check. Retirement moves up the list only when it gets closer at hand.

The changes in rules for finding white-collar work have put financial planning and career management on an equal footing. Flying blind in either instance will not necessarily end in disaster. But by taking appropriate action now, you can improve your chances of successfully navigating the inevitable career turbulence that awaits practically all of us. You need to know certain essential tools for survival. These include:

- Managing the debts on your immediate horizon

- Getting a grip on your cash flow

- Understanding what a real rainy-day fund is—how to set one up and where to keep it

- Realizing the dangers of excessive credit-card use

- Knowing how large a mortgage to take out

These topics provide the basics for thinking ahead in terms of finances. Understanding the steps involved will go a long way toward navigating any financial shoals you run into. You just have to sit down and do it.

What's on Your Immediate Horizon?

Make a list of payments that you intend to do in the short term, which are not now a part of your monthly cash flow considerations. By short term, I mean six months to two years. In some cases, you may want to extend the time period to thirty-six months. These events are farther out, but you can be pretty sure they will happen. An example might be a class reunion trip to another country that is in the planning stage and you intend to participate.

Some people protest that their upcoming horizon is a blank slate. If you really think about it, you'll find that just the opposite is true, because you will discover that it is virtually impossible to look three years into the future and not anticipate some events out of the ordinary. The more you practice developing a horizon list, the better you will get at it. Take a look at the list in Figure B.1 for some typical examples of financial events that are often on someone's immediate horizon that are not included in current expenses.

FIGURE B.1 Immediate horizon list.

ITEMS	MONTHLY COST
Buy a car	_____
Take a trip	_____
Start a rainy-day fund	_____
Buy a flat-screen TV	_____
Buy a computer/printer	_____
Get married	_____
Get divorced	_____
Buy back-to-school clothes and supplies	_____
Take a class	_____
Buy a boat	_____
Start a regular savings plan (401K)	_____
Pay off credit cards	_____
Get a new phone (PDA)	_____
Start student loan payoff	_____

Other things may come to mind, so add them as appropriate. You want to select purchases you are likely to make without either planning ahead or taking the time to see how they affect your month-to-month obligations. Sometimes the decisions are long-term commitments that eventually stretch a person's obligations beyond his or her income, and the individual ends up having to finance the debt obligations using expensive debt instruments and/or lose control of his or her ability to manage emergencies.

Clearly, not all short-term horizon decisions put people in a negative position. Starting to save and/or building an effective rainy-day fund are examples. But they still require funding and need to be taken into consideration as you plan.

By taking the time to understand what is on your immediate horizon, you have gotten through the first phase of any planning situation. Create a regular calendar reminder to revisit the list and change it as your circumstances require. For example, you may decide that buying a new car or taking a trip is not such a good idea, after all. That frequently happens when people begin to make realistic assessments about what they can and cannot afford.

When Bill and Claudia completed their horizon list, they decided they could either borrow the money to pay for their vacation in California or save for it and pay cash. They saved, and as the housing market remained sour, they made a further decision. They took a "stay-cation," something that has become so popular during the Great Recession. Those are shorter trips with a focus on having fun in less expensive ways. They judged the decision a great success. Their series of small trips around the state gave them one of their most memorable summers ever, and they were able to finally save enough to fund that rainy-day account they had put off for far too many years. For the first time they had the financial wherewithal to sock away some money. They became more focused on how much they spent and less on how much they made. A little planning went a long way.

Getting a Grip on Your Cash Flow

Now that you have a good idea of what is on your immediate horizon, let's turn to cash flow. Some people start here, especially when they do not have a clear idea of what they face in the way of coming events. You know that some unexpected problems are always going to come up, like the dishwasher going kaput. The question, then, becomes, Do you have enough cash flow to accommodate the unexpected?

Oscar knew that in two years he would need a new car, and he developed a savings schedule that would give him enough for a sizable down payment. When the time came, his plans were interrupted by a layoff notice. He had the money to go ahead with the purchase, but the timing was wrong. So he delayed buying a car and went job searching, which he concluded in three months. Because his new job came with a sign-on bonus, he now had more options than planned for. On one hand, he could purchase a less expensive car for cash; on the other, he could buy a more expensive car with a sizable down payment. That was a nice luxury that was made possible only because he planned ahead.

The amount of unused cash you have on hand at the end of the month will tell you a lot about how well you will be able to finance future events. It will also tell if you are running a monthly deficit and how it is being financed. That money has to come from somewhere, and people routinely run up their credit cards without thinking. When that method of deficit spending happens month after month, you will rack up an expensive and growing debt that gives little wiggle room when an emergency occurs. Let's see what your cash flow situation looks like.

Cash flow is nothing more than monthly income minus expenses (fixed and variable). The income part is pretty easy to calculate. Your monthly/weekly payroll check stub will tell you exactly how much that is. If your monthly take-home pay is highly variable, calculate your yearly income and divide by twelve.

Use the form in Figure B.2 to calculate your monthly net cash position. Take your time, as the numbers are not always at your fingertips. And if you are seriously off the mark, it will distort your financial situation.

Expenses are trickier, and the tendency for most people is to underestimate them. Here are some helpful hints:

▶ Replacing the tires on your car should be treated as a monthly expense. In accounting terms, they are accrued for and paid out as required. You should do the same.

▶ Utility bills are highly variable. Eliminate the variability by asking the utility companies to supply you with how much you spent last year and divide that into monthly installments. Be sure to set the balance aside anytime the actual payment is less than what you project. It will all balance in the end. Better yet, ask the utility company to put you on a plan whereby your monthly payments are all the same.

▶ You have probably noticed that practically each month brings an unexpected expense—back-to-school clothes for the kids in August, lawnmower repair in May, unplanned trip in October, and so on. They should not be treated as items to be paid for out of your emergency

FIGURE B.2 *Personal cash flow template.*

Personal Cash Flow Template

I. MONTHLY NET INCOME

Salary		
Other		
	Total	

II. EXPENSES

Mortgage		
Utilities		
Auto Loan		
Credit Cards		
1		
2		
3		
Food		
Transportation		
Other Loans		
	Total	

III. MONTHLY CASH FLOW (I MINUS II)

fund. You can plan for them by reviewing your checkbook and credit-card stubs to estimate how much you paid over the course of a full year. Then budget for them. Each month the amount will be different. But then that's the point.

What You Should Know About Credit Cards

We have mentioned credit cards several times, always in a negative light. Actually, they are a wonderful invention. But far too many people get sideways with their credit obligations because they use credit to buy things they otherwise cannot afford. They also tend to think in terms of the incremental monthly amount a purchase will require and not its total cost. When you otherwise can't afford something, it should be a warning sign not to purchase it at all.

Think of it this way. Which would you buy if two perfectly identical items, A and B, were side by side and A had a price tag of $2,000 and B was listed at $3,863? Item A is the obvious choice. Yet when you use a credit card with an 18 percent interest rate and make minimum payments over the life of the loan, you end up paying a full 93 percent more than had you paid cash. The use of credit cards has its place, but their convenience makes it easy to use them without thinking. And when the unexpected emergency happens, you may find that you have very little financial flexibility.

Actually, the A and B example above is somewhat unrealistic because a repayment plan that pays the minimum each month would take over nineteen years to fulfill. None of us would realistically take that long. But we routinely accept thirty-six-month repayment periods. That still means a 30 percent cost premium for using a credit card. You would still buy the $2,000 model over the one costing $2,600.

Another way of looking at the situation is that a credit card is an expensive way to buy things. The less money you have, the more expensive it tends to get because now you're paying off the interest as well as the principle. For that reason, you should avoid using credit cards as a means of purchasing things you cannot otherwise afford. Once you are overextended (and that is easy to do), you limit your ability to purchase other items that are essential. Unless you enjoy washing dishes by hand, or using the laundromat for your clothes, you need to stay out of this trap.

That's not to mention your credit rating. Another difficulty with credit cards is that how you handle them directly feeds your FICO score, a term derived from a company founded by Bill Fair and Earl Isaac in 1956, known as the Fair Isaac Company (FICO). They started selling their assessments of the credit worthiness of individual consumers to the major consumer reporting agencies—Equifax, Experian, Trans Union.

Your FICO score is a weighted assessment of the risk lenders take when they lend you money. The higher the risk, the more it will cost you to borrow. The score is based on the following factors, weighted as indicated:

- *Punctuality* (35%). Whether you pay on time and in agreement with the terms of your contract.

- *Ratio of debt being used to total credit available* (30%). If you are maxed out on your credit cards or anywhere near, it lowers your score.

- *Length of payment history* (15%). Do they have enough credit history on you to pick up on a reliable pattern?

- *Ratio of installment to revolving debt* (10%). Revolving debt is a line of credit made available any time you want to use it (e.g., a credit card); installment debt is where you take out a specific loan amount with a specified term for repayment (mortgages, auto loans). Lenders like to see that you have both, a balanced credit profile.

- *Credit currently applied for* (10%). Mainly the number of credit cards you have applied for; too many lowers your credit score.

FICO scores range from 300 (very bad) to 850 (we doubt anyone has ever seen one that high). Generally, a score of 750 or better will get you the best rates, and anything over 700 is considered very good. You can get by with a score that ranges from 620 to 679, but you will likely be denied credit with a score of 619 or lower.

Go on the Internet to get a free copy of your credit report from each of the credit agencies. Or according to the Federal Trade Commission website you can order your annual free credit report online at annualcreditreport.com, by calling 1-877-322-8228, or by completing the *Annual Credit Report Request Form* and mailing it to Annual Credit Report Request Service, P.O. Box 105281, Atlanta, GA 30348-5281. However, beware of other websites advertising free credit reports that may be fraudulent or turn out not to actually be free.

There will also be instructions on how to fix any errors in the reports and generally how to improve your score. Most debt-counseling services advise you to get your report from all three consumer credit agencies, or at least from two of them, because they often contain different information, some of which may need correction.

Credit-card use has become so ubiquitous in our culture that we have become too casual about how we use them. Consider these suggestions for cutting your dependence on credit cards:

▶ Use credit cards only when carrying cash is inconvenient.

▶ Use your bank debit card instead. That card is tied directly to your checking account, which means you are paying in cash.

▶ Do not extend your monthly cash flow with the use of credit cards.

▶ Pay your credit-card bill in full every month. If you cannot, think about whether you can afford what you have purchased.

There is a good chance you will not be able to pay off your credit-card debt all at once. Yet you can work toward that if you allot a certain sum beyond what you spent in the previous month. If you do, you take another step in the direction of sound financial planning.

When do you teach your kids about the use of credit cards? Many websites help parents teach their children to become financially literate. Enter "teaching the kids about credit" in your browser window, and you will see a whole list of sources pop up. Almost all these services are free and include lesson plans and more general "how-to" instructions about financial literacy for teens. Just make sure you examine the content of the sites before using the material, as some of the information is dated.

CONSIDER PRBC (PAY RENT, BUILD CREDIT)

Millions of Americans are perfectly credit-worthy but without the financial track record sufficient for more standard consideration. That is, their transactions have not been captured and reported to the standard credit rating agencies. They often deal in cash, pay their rent on time, and otherwise are solid credit risks. A new reporting agency (PRBC) was founded in 2002 to capture this population. Individuals can self-enroll to capture their on-time payment patterns and build a solid credit-worthy reputation.

Rainy-Day Funds

Most people have no difficulty understanding how important rainy-day funds can be when a true emergency strikes. But when peril is off in the gauzy future, they have more trouble with this than any other aspect of personal financial planning. If this is true of you, you can take some solace because you are not alone. At one time, forty-seven of fifty state governments had rainy-day funds. The problem is that politicians are attracted to uncommitted piles of budgetary dollars as much as moths are attracted to outdoor lights. The minute the fund is established, the argument starts as to when, where, and how to grab a piece of it. Your own situation won't be any easier. You will likely have a continual debate with yourself and/or your spouse about the funds and how to use them. That's okay. At least you have the money to argue about.

To start, you should understand that rainy-day funds come out of excess revenue. You need to create excess revenue in order to do longer-range financial planning. That is why you took account of events on your immediate horizon; took control of your cash flow; and paid down your credit cards. You are now ready to take a giant step toward financial survival during bouts of unemployment.

The amount of your rainy-day fund should be anywhere from three to six months of net income. Six months is a pretty hefty amount because one of the first things you should do in the event of an emergency (job loss, for example) is to review your variable expenses and cut them back as far as you can. You also have some built-in flexibility by putting off some expenditures that are on your immediate horizon or keeping your fixed expenses under control. Six months' worth of a rainy-day fund could end up funding as much as a year and a half's worth of the funds needed for financial survival. The length of time depends on how seriously you take your personal financial planning.

Do not expect to establish the fund all at once. Work toward your target amount in monthly increments by incorporating savings into your fixed expenses as part of cash flow. You also should make sure these funds are segregated into their own account, used only for a true rainy day. Mixing these monies in with other funds in the same account makes it too easy to access them for purposes for which they were not intended. On the other hand, rainy-day funds should be readily accessible (e.g., in a money market account and not in certificates of deposit, or CDs). You probably will not get much of a return, but that's okay. Remember, you are trying to save rather than make money with this fund. The most important thing is for you to get started.

The Size of Your Mortgage

If you follow the simple steps presented here, before long you will start to think in time frames longer than two to three years. Usually longer-range planning starts with buying a home for the first time, refinancing an existing home, or buying another one. You need to know more about mortgages than will be discussed here. The key fact to understand is that the mortgage company's objective, with a qualified buyer, is to have you take as large a mortgage as you can. It does this by telling you "how much you qualify for," hoping you will use all of it to buy as much house as you can. When houses were rapidly appreciating in value, this wasn't such a bad idea. Now, borrowers need to make sure they do not confuse how much the mortgage company is willing to lend with how much mortgage you can really afford.

You may qualify for an amount that makes you "house poor"—able to service your house debt obligations but little else—or open yourself up to too much exposure in the event of a job loss. To avoid this problem, you can find on the Internet a number of liability calculators that are set up to tell you how much of a mortgage you can afford. On these sites you will learn about the front-end ratio (the percentage of your yearly gross income you can reasonably put toward your principal, interest, taxes, and insurance) and the back-end ratio (the percentage of income needed to cover all your debts). Though there are some differences, the same rules generally apply to both renters and home buyers.

If you have taken the short-term financial planning steps suggested here, this process of calculation will come easily. Mortgages are issued in various shapes, sizes, and monthly payments. To determine how much you can afford, get advice from someone other than real estate and/or mortgage professionals. Their interests in selling you a house and a mortgage do not necessarily align with your interest in sound financial management.

Emergency Planning

You are now ready to answer the question of what you should do if you lose your job. If your short-term financial plan is in place and fully funded, you can conduct your job search with confidence. You likely have enough financial resources and flexibility to transition to your next job comfortably. But you still need to go into emergency-planning mode. More is involved in a layoff than your financial footing. Here is a list of factors you should take into account if you lose your job.

GETTING A GRIP ON YOUR EMOTIONS

People are understandably suspicious when outplacement firms advise them not to take termination personally. After all, outplacement fees are usually paid by the company doing the terminating. When outplacement firms simultaneously advise individuals and the companies, the built-in conflict of interest invariably is resolved in favor of who pays the bill.

You have to face the facts. The laws governing employee/employer relations dramatically favor the employer. In contrast to the industrialized economies of Japan, Germany, France, England, and other countries in Europe, workforce redeployment is not punished—a welcome state if you are a business owner because you can take on and shed workers and their related expenses as desired. Despite some restrictions, the deck is stacked in favor of the employer. In this environment, wrongful-termination lawsuits are iffy propositions that can easily absorb the emotional energy you otherwise need to conduct an effective job search. Most lawsuits of this nature end up being lost in court. A disappointing number of people win awards just large enough to cover their legal fees.

You need to focus on landing a next assignment, and understand that being told you are no longer needed is never a pleasant experience. Experts in the field generally agree that the emotions following a termination develop in five stages—denial, anger, bargaining, depression, and eventually acceptance. You should understand that these emotions are the natural outcome of being terminated. Accepting that employers are often unfair allows you to move on with the rest of your life much sooner.

You should at all times avoid doing and saying precipitous things. Burning bridges is seldom a good idea. Circumstances can change and opportunities for independent work with your same firm may open up down the road. For example, that happened to Bruce, who felt his company should have laid off a lot of other people before it fired him. At first he thought that someone put his name on the list by mistake (denial). He was highly recruited out of college and his performance ratings were always outstanding. Over the next few weeks, a flood of emotions filled his head. Once he was able to impose some structure on what he felt, it became easier to get to acceptance and pour his energy into transition.

The amount of time people take to accept a termination varies. Initially, the objective should be to get a grip on your emotions so you are able to attend to other time-sensitive matters, like focusing on the conditions of your termination.

HOW WERE YOU TERMINATED?

Listen to the conditions of your termination carefully and, if at all possible, get them in writing. Organizations that do not notify you in writing are poorly run, trying to hide something, or both. You should understand the conditions of any severance you have coming, whether it is to be doled out at regular intervals or paid in a lump sum; how long your company-paid benefits will be in force; the status of company life insurance programs, 401(k), and health-care accounts; access to personal records you have kept at your workplace; and what you can expect in the way of outplacement assistance.

You should also request a copy of the company's termination policy. Over the years these have been slimed to entice you to sign a release of liability from the company in exchange for "extra" termination benefits, which most states require for the release to be legally binding. But don't sign or agree to anything before you have had a chance to think for a few days about what just happened, what you may choose to do about it, and what outside advice you may want. For example, retirement accounts may need to be "rolled over" to avoid paying taxes prematurely or incurring early withdrawal penalties. Most reputable financial services firms provide such advice free of charge—not because they are nice guys but because they are eager to get their hands on the transferred funds.

Also, if the clock is ticking on your company-paid benefit program, now may be a good time to schedule dental and doctor's appointments for the entire family. If you have a family lawyer or can access one for a reasonable fee, you may want counsel to review the termination letter to uncover any additional items worth bargaining over. Vacation time, delayed timing on the termination, additional severance, agreed-upon letters of recommendation, and future consideration for reemployment or consulting opportunities are a few of the possibilities you may be able to negotiate or may have been negated in the small print.

TELL FAMILY AND FRIENDS

Telling others of your plight is still difficult to do, but there are some compelling reasons you should push forward. Immediate family members can be great allies who provide emotional support and help in implementing the budget restrictions that may now be necessary. And they may be able to provide some financial support, as well. There is nothing to be embarrassed about. White-collar workers across the board understand job loss and are more accepting than ever. They probably know of others who have gone through job loss, including themselves.

Telling your family and friends is good practice for when you have to talk about your job experiences during the job search. As much as you can, keep emotions out of the account. Avoid talking about what happened in terms of "you against them." At first that will be hard to do, but you will get better at it as you move toward acceptance. You can be sure that if any negativity creeps into your networking or interviewing, it will hurt your future job prospects.

FILE FOR UNEMPLOYMENT BENEFITS

As a practical matter, file for unemployment benefits right away. Processing your application can take as much as four weeks before benefits begin to flow. Also, be aware that any severance will affect your eligibility and may delay when you are eligible to receive benefits.

By filing now, you become familiar with the unemployment rules and regulations and any special programs/services that are available. For example, some states have free Internet access and workplace seminars that may be helpful.

REVISIT YOUR "IMMEDIATE HORIZON" LIST

If you don't have one, put together a list of goals and upcoming needs (see Figure B.2). Anticipated spending should be among the first items you take into consideration. Extra expenditures represent money you would spend that is not currently factored into your monthly cash flow. During the denial stage you may want to pretend nothing has really happened.

"I'm good at what I do and know it. They will be surprised how easily I find another job." This is a particularly dangerous period because you might talk yourself into moving ahead with an expensive purchase just to prove that losing this job is "no big deal." More times than not, that is a serious mistake. Now is a good time to rein in discretionary spending and take care not to take on more credit risk.

Attending a class is the one item on the list that you may want to go ahead with. It could become a part of your job-search strategy to upgrade your skills. In other words, all items on the list should be reviewed, not necessarily eliminated altogether.

CUT YOUR SPENDING

Here is where the rubber meets the road. Your ability to survive long term depends on how much you can cut spending. If you do not have unreasonable levels of debt but have a well-established rainy-day fund and are generally in command of your cash flow, survival is a lot easier. You still have to cut spending, though. Revisit the cash flow exercise and, with the help of your family, look for opportunities to cut.

If you have revolving and installment debt, you may want to consider alerting your creditors about the job situation and negotiate lower payments. The better your credit history, the better the chances that you can negotiate a pretty good deal—or at least a good enough deal to stretch your survival time out long enough to find another job.

Above all, remember that this exercise is not about maintaining your current standard of living. The objective is to cut it down. For instance, when one couple went from a two- to a single-income family, the parents delivered a brand-new lawn mower to their house and announced, "This is your new lawn service contract. Cancel the old one."

Our standard of living usually consists of expensive discretionary items we can do without—daily visits to Starbucks, monthly haircuts, air-conditioned houses, prepared foods from the grocery store, eating out regularly, and a lot more when you really put your mind to all the time-saving aspects of a busy life. For the time being, you're not nearly as busy, are you?

Launch a Job Search

No one really knows how this worldwide restructuring of the workforce is going to play out. You can be sure, however, that the competition for jobs of all kinds, especially white-collar jobs, will continue to rise. So you should prepare for an even more competitive workplace. You have started to do that by reading *Cracking the New Job Market*. Others who have done so have found work and continued along a career path that makes them happy, whether they changed careers or stayed the course. In all cases they learned that getting a job was never so much about them as about what others wanted from them. Creating value became the basis for effective career management.

You have all the tools right in your hand. Now it's your turn!

• • • • • • • • • • *Things to Remember* • • • • • • • • •

▸ *Now, more than ever, financial management and career planning go hand in hand. Workforce and job instability makes financial planning a necessity.*

▸ *Figure out those items that are on your immediate horizon—what they cost and how you intend to pay for them. Good financial planning starts there.*

▸ *Calculate your cash flow. That knowledge helps you to refrain from inadvertently funding a growing monthly shortfall. It also allows you to begin that all-important rainy-day fund.*

▸ *Credit-card debt is expensive and should be avoided. If you become over-extended, it affects your credit worthiness (your FICO score) and limits financial flexibility when you need it most.*

▸ *Rainy-day funds come from excess cash. The funds should be kept segregated from other funds and be easy to access in the event of an emergency. Like everyone else, you will likely struggle with deciding when to use them.*

▶ As you turn your attention to more long-term considerations, remember not to confuse what a mortgage lender is willing to lend you with what you can afford. Consult one of the numerous calculators available on the Internet.

▶ If you lose your job, you should have already done the necessary financial planning to bridge to the next job opportunity. Whether you have or not, now is the time for emergency planning. Get a grip on your emotions, tell family and friends, file for unemployment benefits, revisit your "immediate horizon" list, cut spending, and launch your job search.

NOTES

1. Deloitte KnowledgeCo LLC and Harrison Group, "The 2010 American Pantry Study," www.deloitte.com/us/americanpantrystudy.

2. Ken Little, *Personal Finance Desk Reference* (New York: Alpha Books, 2007), p. 2.

Applying the Job-Search Rules to Worldwide Employment

I RECENTLY CAME across a headline from an online student publication that read, "Job Security Is a Thing of the Past."[1] The sentiment expressed was familiar—it is a difficult job market for college graduates in this generation.

Was this written by an American student facing an uncertain circumstance? It does not take much to imagine that it also could have been written by a student almost anywhere else in the world—Mexico, Canada, Europe, China, Japan, or perhaps India. The comment is actually from a recent college graduate from Gaborone, Botswana, which is one of the fastest-growing cities in the world. Obviously, the new rules of the job marketplace apply worldwide, not just to white-collar professionals in the United States or other developed countries. The question is less whether the same rules apply everywhere and more about which rules apply and in what way. This appendix is intended to share some initial thoughts on that situation.

The Benefits of a College Education

The political, business, and educational leadership of countries around the world recognize that participation in the global economy requires an educated workforce. And their individual citizens are motivated by the same promises given to American workers for the past several decades: go to college, get a job, and become upwardly mobile.

Supportive public policies combined with prospects of personal upward mobility have provided powerful incentives. China, for example, now churns out more than 6.3 million college graduates a year—up dramatically from just a few years ago. Many of these students are from impoverished rural towns. They went to college in the provinces, believing that studying hard would bring them better lives as compared with their parents. We now know that many of these newly minted college graduates worldwide will be disappointed—a lot of them because their degrees alone have not made them as competitive in the job market as they need to be. Does the college degree still guarantee a better life? They, too, are asking, "Now that I have my degree, where is my career?"

In truth, professional workers everywhere are subject to the same forces of globalization and changes in technology. They all would benefit from information that shows them how to crack the new job market and survive the instability that is now an inherent part of the global workforce. The mobility of jobs across national boundaries has created an ebb and flow of opportunities with differential impacts. Jobs that flow from the United States to India, for example, create short-term opportunities for one group to the apparent detriment of another group. The people of India will eventually be dismayed to discover that jobs can flow out of India as easily as they have flowed in.

Though the urgency is occasionally offset by an influx of opportunities in any one country, the expectation is that competition for professional jobs everywhere will continue to increase, fueled by globalization and a growing population of professional workers with similarly rising expectations. Striking the right balance between the availability of professional workers and the number of job opportunities will be difficult.

The integration of China and India alone into the global economy represents a 70 percent expansion of the global labor force.[2] In the 1990s, once the educational and political leadership in China recognized the link between the new economy and education, it doubled the openings at Chinese universities. Unfortunately, the numbers of newly degreed students in China continue to far outpace the job market for these college graduates. White-collar professionals are commonly referred to as the new "underclass" of smart, young, and impoverished workers squeezed by China's lower wages and the higher cost of city living. Many of that country's professionals prefer "red-collar" jobs—working for the government—because of their more stable wage scale.

India has its own set of problems, with only 30 percent of its universities, 16 percent of its colleges, and 10 percent of its management institutes receiving accreditation. According to various estimates, the quality of education is thought to be so poor that "Indian students spend about $7 billion to go abroad and study in foreign universities because of the poor quality of education at home. As high as 86 percent of students in science and technology, who obtain degrees in the US, don't return."[3] Though India has captured a leadership position in the global information-technology and business-process outsourcing arenas, it will need to dramatically improve the quality of its graduates to maintain that position. That is because better products at better costs require correspondingly higher levels of educational attainment. Yet, it has been estimated that because of the quality of its educational system, fewer than 25 percent of India's technical graduates are employable.[4]

In China, India, and elsewhere, individuals with rising expectations are pushing to get whatever education they can. Over time, countries will work out their own solutions to these employment problems. But the job and career needs of individuals aren't met over time; just as for American students, they happen right now, and extend into the near future. Individuals everywhere want to know how to crack the new job market. This book's seven rules for getting hired are applicable to their situation.

How Professionals Worldwide Can Use This Book

Keep in mind that this book is about how to find a job and how to manage your career. Don't wait until you are on the wrong side of the worldwide ebb and flow of professional jobs. When the tide is against more opportunities in a given country, perfectly qualified people will have difficulty finding suitable work. Even when the opportunities are relatively abundant, there will be intense competition for higher-paying jobs. So, there is no better time than right now to learn which rules apply in other countries and how to use them.

Five of the rules presented in this book in particular have currency regardless of your country of citizenship. But be sure to pay attention to the context in which the rules exist. You will know better than others how the particulars of each rule are influenced by considerations of culture, politics, and your legal system. Those considerations notwithstanding, use the following advice to get the most out of your situation.

Rule #1: Always Demonstrate Your Value

Today's job-application process requires that you first take note of the particular problems an organization is trying to solve in filling the position. Then make sure that whoever reviews your credentials knows you have solved those problems before and can do it again. Notice that I did not say "whoever reads your résumé." Western-style résumés don't work in all cultures. Whatever the process happens to be, you need to demonstrate your value to the organization. Even when you have no experience, at least you can demonstrate that you have the skills the company is looking for in an entry-level position.

Getting hired will not make your job secure; however, you now have a major advantage over competitors because you understand how the new job market works and how to make it function for you. Globalization and advances in technology have heightened the reliance businesses have on employees who can create value, regardless of location. Demands of greater global competition make companies eager to hire employees who can help them achieve results. In this global economy, the jobs come and go, so it is better to learn how to handle instability than to look for employers who will not outsource.

Similarly, the Internet has introduced near-instant communication across the globe, reducing the cost of data transmission and product distribution to near zero; making price data for an endless variety of goods and services readily available, thereby driving down prices and profit margins; reducing the barriers to entry for niche businesses; and generally intensifying global competition. Jobs can now exist long distances from their primary markets, making them feasible anywhere the goods and services can be produced at the desired cost and quality.

Though businesses are reluctant to terminate employees who create value, the true advantage of value creation is not the protection one gets against termination. By stressing value creation you create a value that is marketable to others as well. Once you learn to create value in this context, you deepen your understanding of how the job market works and how to navigate it.

Rule #2: Your Résumé: It's About the Value You Create

The first step in successfully navigating the job market is to produce a compelling application or résumé. This is most easily accomplished when you understand that your application or résumé is not about you—it is about what others want from you. And you can discover what that is by using an educated eye to review the requirements for the job for which you are applying, the company's website, and industry publications. Then follow the five steps outlined below:

1. Identify the key words employers use in the position description to describe the value they want. Key words clarify the skills an employer is looking for in a new hire, as well as identifying the issues a company is currently facing. Highlight all the action verbs, adjectives, and skills that refer to the attributes the employer is seeking. Also, identify key words on the employer's website and in industry publications.

2. List your relevant job experiences in reverse chronological order. Here is where you *begin* the focus on your background. These job experiences are important, but the output from this exercise is not your résumé itself. Alas, this is where many people end as they prepare to find a new job; by stopping here, they fail to infuse their résumés with value, ending up with an unfocused document that is not tied to the value an employer is asking to have created. That is, their résumés are written without taking the interests of the employer into consideration.

3. Infuse your experiences with value. That is, quantify and qualify your job experiences and insert words and phrases that match the key words identified above. *Quantitative* results include numerical indicators, such as dollar figures;

these are generally recognized as expressions of value. When specific, quantitative results are not possible to give, substitute *qualitative* results, such as "first place," "top ranked," or "1 out of xx." The language of value creation can also be derived from the key words in the position description, the company's website, and industry publications. Use that language to describe your accomplishments. It is language the employer will understand.

4. Select the best statements. The best statements are ones that illustrate specific value you have created and that reflect the prospective employer's needs, as expressed in the position description or elsewhere.

5. Format and refine your résumé. The two basic types of résumés are the reverse chronological (preferred for most applications) and the functional. Examples of both are included in this book. Instructions and examples for the different sections of a résumé are provided, along with sample handbills and cover letters. Sample résumés for entry-level, mid-level, and senior-level positions are also provided.

Once you have developed a customized résumé for one position, you are ready to conduct a full-fledged job search. Remember to customize your résumé for each position you apply for. That's not as difficult as it sounds because there will be considerable overlap from one job to another, especially for those in the same industry. For specific examples, refer to Rule #2 in the book.

Rule #3: Use Social Media and Other Sites for Job Leads

Today's employers need cost-effective ways to execute their talent-acquisition functions. Traditionally, there has not been an agreed-upon methodology, and many openings went unadvertised. This led some people to speculate about the existence of a "hidden job market." Lately, the job-search process has been greatly influenced by social-networking sites, which have shown job markets to be more splintered than hidden. Increasingly, those searching for talent use the Internet as their core methodology, making job openings more visible and less costly to fill. Similarly, individuals have begun to use social-networking techniques to locate jobs and connect with companies. American job seekers are counseled to use

LinkedIn, Facebook, and Twitter as their starting points. Of those, only LinkedIn is specifically designed to facilitate connectivity among business professionals. Using Twitter and Facebook for a job search requires slightly more imagination; more generally, you can use them to connect with others and exchange networking ideas. In fact, you will be surprised how many people are willing to provide useful information as you conduct a job search. Review the discussion of social networking in this book and do some Internet brainstorming, bending the popular social-networking sites to serve your purposes.

According to the technology blog ReadWriteWeb.com (as of June 2009), the following are the top three networking sites for the countries listed:[5]

- Australia: Facebook, MySpace, Twitter

- Canada: Facebook, MySpace, Flickr

- India: Facebook, Orkut, Hi5 (Twitter is a close fourth)

- France: Facebook, Skyrock, MySpace

- China: QQ, Xiaonei, 51

- Germany: Facebook, StudiVz, MySpace

- Italy: Facebook, Netlog, Badoo

- Russia: V Kintakte, Odnoklassniki, LiveJournal

- Spain: Facebook, Tuenti, Fotolog

- United Kingdom: Facebook, Bebo, MySpace

- United States: Facebook, MySpace, Twitter

You will notice that LinkedIn is not listed; however, the site is strongly recommended. It is present in over 200 countries, with executives from all the Fortune 500 companies as members and over 14 million unique visitors per month; the site is devoted to servicing the needs of business professionals.

Rule #4: Interviews: They're About the Value You Demonstrate

Most of what has been discussed earlier in the book pertains to international situations as well, with the exception of protocols. These basics of etiquette are culturally based and vary on such things as being on time and what that really means, appropriate attire for men and women, what to take to the interview, how to manage references, and expected follow-up in anticipation of next steps. In many countries, Western-style business dress for men and women is still appropriate.

The discussion in this book covers the different kinds of interviews, including one-on-ones, interviewing during meals, the use of assessments, group competitions, good cop/bad cop trickery, and telephone and video interviews. As regards the questions themselves, know that much of your preparation work has been done, and that answers to these interview questions are handled the same, in that they are opportunities to talk about things of interest to the interviewer.

What are the interviewers interested in? They want to know how your experiences fit with the value they are seeking to have created when they fill the position for which you are applying. And where do you find that information? It is stated in the position description, on the company's website, and in industry publications—the very same places you looked for information to produce your value-infused résumé. In other words, preparing for interviews is an extension of the résumé-writing process.

The interview, as with your résumé, is not about you. It is about what others want from you. And the book's discussion of methodology shows you the way to give that to them. You can consult the book's numerous examples for using the same format to answer different questions. You can use the special tips for discussing personal developmental needs, gaps in employment, reasons for leaving your last job, conflicts with fellow employees, and salary requirements. Remember, though, that these types of questions will be influenced by the cultural norms of the country involved.

Rule #5: You Get What You Negotiate, Not What You Deserve

Once you get an offer of employment, make sure you get everything you want—before you accept the offer. Make a list early in the job-search process of conditions or benefits you need or want in your next job. Divide your list into three parts:

"must have," "would like to have," and "would like to have but can do without." This "flat" sort of priorities can be your general (nonrigid) guide during the job search. Keeping your priorities front and center is important as you negotiate, weighing those things that are most important and sacrificing things of less importance. Having the list handy provides clarity in the heat of negotiation.

You negotiate when you are in your most powerful position, which is after an offer has been extended but before it is accepted. The rules for skillful negotiation were identified in the book, but international negotiations often take a different tack. Subtleties from one culture to the next constitute important differences, so be careful in how you apply these rules:

1. *Know how you stack up against the competition.* You are in a more powerful position if you are the only candidate for a critical opening. (As stated previously, this information can be difficult to get.)

2. *Underplay your hand.* Rather than bargaining for all of your priorities as if they were of equal importance, show a willingness to be flexible, especially when it comes to those you "would like to have but can do without."

3. *Once on the job, underpromise and overdeliver.* If you continually set goals you cannot meet, your performance will not match expectations. Be both thoughtful and firm in negotiating your performance goals. Remember, the negotiation game never ends.

NOTES

1. "Job Security Is a Thing of the Past: Advice for Aspiring Jobseekers in Gabscity," www.Gabscity.com.

2. Lael Brainard, "Meeting the Challenge of Income Instability," Brookings Institution, February 28, 2007, http://www.brookings.edu/testimony/2007/0228 labor_brainard.aspx.

3. "What Ails Higher Education in India?" IndCareer.com, http://www.indcareer. com/news/what-ails-higher-education-india#.

4. "Executive Summary: Extending India's Global Leadership of the Global IT and BPO Industries," NASSCOM-McKinsey Report, available at www.mckinsey.com/ideas/articles/indialeadership.asp.

5. Doug Coleman, "Social Networks Around the World," June 7, 2009, http://www.readwriteweb.com/archives/post_2.php#.

Example of a Functional Résumé

FRANCIS D. NICHOLS

708 Winthrop Drive	Home 317-555-7009
Simpson, Minnesota 45537	Cell 317-555-9007
	frank.nichols@sbcglobal.net

EXECUTIVE SUMMARY

Accomplished P&L manager and business development executive with substantial experience in public and governmental affairs, corporate communications, human resources consulting, and law. Exceptional negotiator and communicator with proven team-building and leadership skills. International business experience in Russia, the Pacific Rim, West Africa, Mexico, Brazil, and Canada. Expertise in hiring the right people and leading staff to understand and embrace organization's vision to produce success.

SELECTED CAREER HIGHLIGHTS

General Management

- Was directly accountable for developing and implementing market strategy, selecting and training key employees, coordinating workflow, forecasting/budgeting revenue, and controlling costs.

- Reengineered three-state Pacific Northwest market; grew revenues by 34.9% over 3-year period; improved profit margins by 50%.

- Grew tristate Southwest market by 43% over 3-year period; profitability improved by 11%. Market share grew from estimated 14% to 33% over same period.

‣ Reduced operating costs by 31% in a challenging business climate with resultant net profit contribution of 8% over Plan.

Business Development

‣ Led elite sales team responsible for large-scale global transactions. Responsibilities included direction of RFP response strategy, client presentation, and negotiation of terms and global pricing.

‣ Accounted for 24% of the firm's global revenue with win rate that exceeded 70% in competitive bid setting.

‣ Won sizable multiyear exclusive agreement with Fortune 500 energy company resulting in long-term satisfied customer and improvement of revenues and profit to company.

‣ Converted from a preferred to exclusive provider agreement with international natural resource company and expanded other line-of-business service offerings. Resulted in quadrupling of annual revenues from account.

Strategic Planning

‣ Identified opportunities to strategically move business units beyond current company success profiles. Established new directions that challenged accepted business practices and managed the risks to improve profitability.

‣ Selected as one of ten (out of 10,000 employees) to serve on blue-ribbon corporate energy-related strategic planning task force utilizing scenario-based planning (Stanford Research Institute principles). Focused on government regulation as primary business driver that would define company's role both as significant energy user and as supplier. Senior Management ultimately merged company's coal and oil and gas operations into one comprehensive energy business.

‣ Developed innovative marketing strategy to sell both coal and natural gas to utility and large industrial energy customers by taking advantage of deregulation of natural gas, changes in interstate pipeline regulation, and emissions trading permitted under the Clean Air Act Amendment.

Communications, Investor Relations, Government Affairs, Law

‣ Substantial experience and proven track record corporate communications; global investment strategies; print and electronic media; employee communications/community relations; and international, federal, state, and local governmental affairs.

‣ Provided leadership in company's drive to position itself with key stakeholders through corporate communications, identification of programs focusing on company's commitment to environmental excellence, and partnerships with communities and host governments.

‣ Designed and directed sustainable development community programs for mining projects in third world countries.

‣ Initiated regular face-to-face meetings with investment constituencies resulting in increased information flow between company, large investors, and industry analysts.

> ‣ Advocated company policy before Congress, federal regulatory agencies, and several state governments on energy, environment, public lands, corporate tax, and health and safety issues. Resulted in advancement of government policy that positively affected company's profitability.

> ‣ Chaired industry task force on global climate change and successfully lobbied against unilateral CO_2 reduction and carbon tax, thereby saving company millions of dollars for its coal, oil and gas, and aluminum business units.

WORK HISTORY

Right Management Consultants, Philadelphia, Pennsylvania   **1998–2006**
A worldwide leader in human capital consulting (formerly traded on NYSE)

Senior Vice President—Global Response Team, Houston, Texas (2005–2006)

Regional Managing Principal—West Region, Houston, Texas (2004–2005)

Managing Principal—Southwest Market, Houston, Texas (2002–2004)

Managing Principal—Northwest Market, Seattle, Washington (1999–2002)

Managing Director—Washington and Alaska, Seattle, Washington (1998–1999)

Echo Bay Mines, Ltd., Denver, Colorado   **1995–1997**
International Gold Mining Company

Vice President—Communications and Investor Relations (1997)

Director—Government Affairs (1995–1997)

Amax, Inc., New York, New York   **1975–1994**

Director—Marketing Services, Amax Gas Marketing, Inc., Houston, Texas (1992–1994)

Senior Counsel—AMAX, Inc., Washington, DC (1985–1992)

Various legal and regulatory analysis positions, Indianapolis, Indiana (1975–1985)

EDUCATION

Juris Doctor, Indiana University School of Law—Indianapolis
Bachelor of Arts, Political Science, cum laude, Ball State University

INDEX